GOD HAS A PLAN
FOR THE
UNDERDOG

To: Jeff

[signature]

Ps. 34:8

SHELLEY "BUTCH" ANTHONY III

Jesus & Butch Publishing Company

Printed in the United States of America.

ISBN: 978-0-9992198-0-5

Library of Congress Number: 2017911841

GodHasAPlanForTheUnderdog.com

God Has a Plan for the Underdog

By
Shelley "Butch" Anthony III
Owner, This Is It! Bar-B-Q and Seafood

Contents

Dedication

It is with utmost humility and eternal gratitude that I dedicate this book to my loving parents, the late Shelley Anthony II and Lillian Anthony. To my father, I would say, "Thank you for being my hero, the one I looked up to." Likewise, to my mother, "Thank you for letting me know that I was born to be a king." Collectively, my parents planted a seed within me that God has seen fit to cultivate and bring me to this point in my life. Therefore, my heart is full of love, joy, and gratitude as I dedicate this book to the earthly parental heritage that God chose to bestow upon me.

Acknowledgements

A widely-held belief is that no man is an island in and of himself. In addition, when it comes to the colossal task of chronicling one's life story, this belief only gains more credibility. To that end, I would like to take this time to thank my team for helping to make this all possible.

First and foremost, I thank my Lord and Savior, Jesus Christ, for thinking enough of me and trusting me enough to birth the business concept that He has given me. I thank Him also for giving me the fortitude to share my story with the world. Without Him, I am nothing and I most certainly could do nothing.

I would like to thank my family for all their love and support during this journey. My wife, Diane, is a constant source of support. Sometimes the long hours I've had to put in the business cut my time with her short, but she's always been understanding. I also appreciate my children for all their work in the business and for being by my side. Whether in good times or bad, they've stuck with me when they could have been doing something else.

I offer special thanks to my editorial team: Alonia Jones for her exceptional writing and editing skills and Melinda Sylvester for her incomparable ability to help assure that everything flows as it should. Additional gratitude is also in order to David Gary, Paula Palmer

Green, and Nakoreya Roberson for their individual artistic gifts that were so graciously rendered for this project. Their collective efforts have produced the work that you now hold in your hands.

Additionally, I would like to thank my pastor, Bishop Dale C. Bronner, an extraordinary man of God. As well, I am equally appreciative for the many prayer partners who have gone to God with me and through intercession.

Last but certainly not least, I would like to express my appreciation for the This Is It! management team and the many employees who have been part of the team through the years. The commitment and loyalty that they have shown to my family and the business will always be remembered.

With gratitude,

Shelley "Butch" Anthony III

Foreword

You hold in your hand a compelling work that proves that little can become much when you put it in the Master's hand! This is not only a unique, passionate story of rags to riches, but of tragedy to triumph and of disappointment to deliverance. The story of Shelley "Butch" Anthony III is an inspiring account of how the ordinary can become extraordinary with faith in God, a clear vision, hard work, and determination! As you follow his journey, you'll discover that it was not always easy. There were many bumps in the road. There was frustration, sickness, disappointment, betrayal, hurt and even unexpected death. Yet, through it all, he never gave up!

I am personally proud of Butch and how God has graced him to do so much over time, starting with so little! To see his humility is quite refreshing to me. He has walked with presidents, yet has not lost the common touch! He has been faithful with a little, and God has entrusted him with more. The steps of Butch's life have been ordered by the Lord. Like a child, he has depended on God, and God has been faithful to bring him through every challenge! He has proven that every weakness we have is an opportunity for God to show His strength in our life.

Butch's life reminds me of the biblical passage which says, "Remember, dear brothers and sisters, that few of you were wise in the world's eyes or powerful or wealthy when God called you. Instead, God chose things the world considers foolish in order to shame those who think they are wise. And he chose things that are powerless to shame those who are powerful. God chose things despised by the world, things counted as nothing at all, and used them to bring to nothing what the world considers important. As a result, no one can ever boast in the presence of God" (I Cor. 1:26-29 NLT).

Butch had a good father who laid a great foundation for him. What blossomed so beautifully in his life was really part of his heritage from his father. In places where his dad walked, Butch has run! Perhaps now in places where Butch has run, his children will fly! But it is wonderful to see that he has not given in to a generation that is marked by a sense of "entitlement." To the contrary, Butch has taught his family members to have a strong work ethic, and that nothing in life is free! They have been given an opportunity to work hard and earn their way.

The invaluable, practical life lessons that you'll learn from Butch's story will empower you and equip you to live at a higher level. If God could do it in Butch's life, He can do it in yours! After reading this book, you'll realize, "I now have no excuse!" So get ready to be blasted out of your comfort zone into your significance zone! Your greatest days are ahead! Destiny awaits!

Bishop Dale C. Bronner, D. Min.

Founder/Senior Pastor

Word of Faith Family Worship Cathedral

Prologue

A Salute to My Husband

Congratulations to my husband for being the strong and courageous man of God that he is. Obedience to God has always been his heart's desire. My husband's motto is, "Out of all that I do, I just don't want to disappoint God." So to God be the glory for Butch's obedience in saying yes to God by writing this book.

Our family is so proud of Butch's spiritual walk and his strong work ethic, which have spread to his kids, his co-workers, business associates, and people that don't know him. My husband has shown loyalty, commitment, integrity, and dedication, not only to me, but also to everything that is meaningful in his life. He has even exhibited these qualities to the people with whom he has only had short acquaintances. When God speaks, he moves. He is a rock that crumbles not under pressure; he yet stands strong and tall through it all.

Years ago, the doctor assumed that Butch had a heart attack. After tests were completed, the doctor made a comment about his heart that I shall never forget. He said that he has a heart like a baboon, meaning it's strong and healthy. Achieving all that he has accomplished truly has been a struggle: a struggle that keeps him up at night; a struggle that will make him cry sometimes; a struggle that tries his faith; a struggle that tried his integrity; a struggle that will cause you to become fearful. But God has kept him from them all.

My husband has truly been through the fire. By going through the fire, he has developed into the kind of man that would make any woman wish that he was theirs. A child only dreams of a dad like him. Any man will want his qualities of bravery, strength and the boldness to go for what he wants. A mother would adore him as her son. A father would brag with a proud heart who his son is. What a man! If I had the power, I would clone him, and my daughters would have wonderful husbands. People would say that the Anthony's girls are so blessed.

One day when I went to my nail shop, I looked up and noticed a picture of a lady in this big plush chair. Around her were people giving her different types of services. The script at the bottom of the picture said, "It's good to be a queen." I took a deep breath, smiled, and said, "That's me, a queen."

When my husband became born again, his love for me changed. It became clear that the change was that he was all the more deeply in love with me. The love he shows for me reflects a sacrifice in his life daily so that I can have a fulfilled life until the time of my death. Whenever he publicly speaks – and it matters not if it is an audience of two people or 2,000 people – he boldly acclaims me as, "My wife, whom I refer to as my queen." We share a love that only God has put together. Men and women have tried, but they have been powerless in their attempts to separate our love for one another.

My husband saw me first and pursued me. Two years later, we were united as Mr. & Mrs. Shelley Anthony III. Now I tell my kids they are so blessed because I found them the best dad!

I look up to my husband with pure reverence in regards to all that he is and all that he wants to be. My prayer for him is that God will bless him all the days of his life.

With love, respect, and admiration,

Barbara Diane Anthony

Introduction

Underdog. It's not a pretty word because of its lack of magnetism. It's not a word that very many people would have the courage to identify themselves as such. Such is not my testimony. As a Black man in America who sprang from humble beginnings and lived in a society that had already predetermined my chances of success would be slim to none, there was a time when I was, indeed, considered the underdog....at least by the world's standards, that is.

However, I serve a higher power. His name is Jesus Christ. Every aspect of my life is undergirded by what He has made known to me through His Word, the Holy Bible. I have been particularly encouraged by Jeremiah 29:11, which says, "For I know the plans I have for you, declares the Lord. Plans to prosper you and not to harm you, plans to give you hope and a future." I interpret that as being God knew me first; before my MuhDear knew my daddy, God knew me and had a plan for my life. Therefore, I can truly say that the scripture I just referenced is not a threat; it's a promise. It's a promise I have chosen to believe, and it's a promise I have chosen to stand on wholeheartedly.

I am Shelley "Butch" Anthony III. By the grace of God, I am a blessed and highly favored man. This Is It! BBQ and Seafood has a wonderful legacy that spans 65 years. Our empire boasts of eight corporate stores and one franchise (at the time of publishing), a state-of-the-art events center, catering services, national media coverage for specialty food cuisine, and national recognition as consumers' choice for "Best BBQ". We are excited to have introduced our new franchise program. In the eyes of everyday people, it may be surmised that these accomplishments represent a glorious life. I see it as the glory of what God has done. Yet, what few people realize are the inevitable challenges, trials and tribulations that were endured so that the manifestation of what currently exists to be reality. To put it in terms of familiarity, let me just say, "You see the glory, but you really don't know the story."

This testament of "the story" can be paralleled to the production of music and food: it's all a process. For example, when we listen to music, all we are primarily concerned about is the final product that speaks a universal language to our hearts and souls. We are excitedly waiting to hear that melodious sound that makes us smile, sing, and dance. Yet, most people rarely take into consideration all the steps that must be taken so that everything can come together. Lyrics have to be written, music has to be composed, voices have to be added, and it all has to go through a full process called production. In essence, with any major undertaking, people see and enjoy the final product. Accordingly, they see the glory, but they may not necessarily know the story or feel the pain that was such a very real part of the journey.

In the same manner, it's no secret that a basic fundamental of life is food. We know that food is necessary for the sake of nourishing our bodies. How often do we pause to think about the many processes that must take place in order for our bodies to be nourished and our taste buds to be tantalized? It matters not if it's meat, vegetables, bread, or liquid. Anything we put into our bodies must first go through a process.

The same principle of process just described for music and food are not absent factors when it comes to success. I guarantee you that if you study the life of one who has achieved any measure of success, there has been a major process along the way. And such a process is no walk in the park, I might add. In fact, I'll go as far as to suggest that such processes began with dreams for a great destiny, yet faced the unanticipated realities that were soiled with struggles, fertilized with failures, and watered with weariness. I can say this because I know exactly what I'm talking about; I am no exception. These are not simply flowery words. Instead, they are words that have become truth by way of personal experience. I know what it is to be disappointed, to make mistakes, and simply to want to give up. I know what it is to put in a hard day's work only to come home and find all your belongings sitting out on the street. Yes, eviction is one of the many life's disappointments I have had to face.

Yet, here I stand today. Who would have ever dreamed that a Black boy from Tampa, Florida – one who closed the door on education in the 10th grade, one who struggled with many of life's addictions, one who faced personal struggles, one who had countless discouragers who said he would never make it – would still land on his feet and sit at the helm of a company that has earned a national reputation as its industry's best? It may sound and seem impossible, but that's exactly what God has done for me!

The pages you are about to read will unveil the journey of my life from my earliest existence. This Is It! Bar-B-Q and Seafood is a true testimony of the infinite possibilities that can unfold when there is vision, hope and faith in God. As I candidly open my heart and take you down the numerous avenues traveled as I moved from dream to destiny, I truly hope you will understand that God really does have a plan for the underdog. I pray that this chronicle will cause you to dream big or, better yet, dream bigger. Perhaps, it will inspire you to rekindle the flame of a dream deferred. Whatever your response may be, I, in all humility, want you to know that all things really are possible with God.

Finally, as you prepare to hear my story, I'd like to share these God-inspired words of wisdom from my pastor, Bishop Dale C. Bronner, "In every failure resides opportunity. There is an opportunity to learn, to grow, to teach, to do and be better. Some form of failure always precedes success. Embrace the challenge. Take a risk. Fail forward. Be bold. Opportunity awaits." I can most certainly testify to the benefits of embracing the challenge that opportunity presents. I've taken many risks. I have failed forward. I have been bold. As a result, I was greeted by a world of opportunity that causes me to inspire others to believe that they, too, can overcome anything and walk in their life's purpose. If you are looking forward to reading a true to life story illuminating the fact that dreams really can come true, THIS IS IT! I embrace Psalm 34:8 "O, taste and see..." as a true testament of God's goodness to and through This Is It! To God be all the glory!

Sincerely,

Shelley "Butch" Anthony III

Chapter 1

Tampa: The Place Where the Plan Began

I am Shelley "Butch" Anthony III. Many may see my name and immediately associate me with the chain of restaurants that God has entrusted to me and my family's care. By His grace, This Is It! Bar-B-Q and Seafood has achieved a measure of success that greatly exceeds anything my mother and father could have ever dreamed of when they started Anthony's Drive-Inn in 1951. I am fully persuaded that they unknowingly began a legacy that is still alive and well today. I stand amazed and in total humility about the wondrous works God has done. I will forever give Him praise.

Regardless of the perceived success, it must be clearly understood that everything and everyone has a beginning. For me, the beginning took place in a city called Tampa, located on the west coast of Florida. More specifically, I was born in what is called West Tampa. I am the first surviving child (of seven) born to Shelley and Lillian Anthony, two hard working people who wanted, like many Americans, to fulfill the American Dream. They wanted to make a decent living and lay a foundation for their family to do the same. As I matured in my Christian walk, I began to understand laying such a foundation could become a reality according to Matthew 6:33, which says, "But seek ye first the kingdom of God, and His righteousness; and all these things shall be added unto you."

My father was a good man. While he was not perfect – no one is – he was a good role model. He always carried himself with self-respect. Never did I hear him curse, and he kept himself clean cut and well-dressed at all times. He loved his family, and he had no problem with showing love for us. I'll never forget how he always wanted his boys (my younger brother, LaGrant, and I) to be with him. Many times, he'd take us to the warehouse with him to shop for items needed at the restaurant.

Being an entrepreneur in a day and age where such a thing was not so common, favorable, or even equitable for Black people, my father laid the foundation for what I can now attribute my work ethic. Hands down, he was one of the hardest working men we had ever seen. He worked all the time, only getting five to seven hours of sleep each night. He had to do it that way because, as the owner of a 24-hour restaurant, he had to break his sleep and check to make certain the operations of each shift were intact. He checked everything from the money to the cleanliness to the staffing. Totally committed to excellent service in every way, it was essential for everything to be on point.

My father only had a 4th or 5th grade education, but he never allowed that to be a barrier to setting and achieving his goal of running a successful business. It would not suffice for him only to gain enough to get what he called a "knot in his pocket," which meant the accumulation of a good bit of money earned. Instead, he wanted to generate enough that would create a lasting legacy; a solid foundation upon which his children could build, become self-sufficient, and live an honorable lifestyle. He was an excellent example that anything can be done with hard work and determination.

Just as my father was a good man, so was my mother a good woman. It's no secret that there's nothing like a mother's love. Some would even say that a person's mother is their very first teacher. I would agree because there is so much that we learned from our mother. First, and foremost, she was always there for us. She was a mother like no other. This is something that LaGrant and I don't take for granted. You see, our dear mother (whom we affectionately called MuhDear) had seven boys. However, she suffered five miscarriages while working at the restaurant. LaGrant and I are survivors because we were the ones she was able to deliver to full term. God allowed us to defeat the odds. Neither of us will ever be able to thank God enough for that.

We feel tremendously blessed by having the mother God gave us. She made our house a home. It was always good to come home to a clean house and cooked food. She could cook better than anyone in the world! She could make simple dishes seem so special. One of her favorites was chicken and rice. Another was crab shilah (which some people may refer to as crab shiloh). This is a Spanish dish made from blue crabs and tomato sauce.

Not only was our mother an excellent cook, but she also taught us to cook. Under her watchful and loving tutelage, we learned by doing. In addition to being a wonderful cook and passing her gift of cooking to us, our mother was also an avid swimmer. She could swim an entire lake – Walker's Lake – without getting her hair wet. This was a huge lake, so imagine that! I used to be afraid for her to swim the lake because I feared she would be attacked by the alligators. I vividly remember my Aunt Sweetie telling me how MuhDear went fishing in the lake when she was pregnant with LaGrant. She said she fell out the boat and that the alligators smelled her "pregnant woman scent." Thank God, she got away. She was a great swimmer, and this is something she taught us to do as well.

In addition to the love we received from our parents, we were also blessed to have the presence of our Aunt Dot, our father's sister, in our life. While we are grateful to have grown up and developed a relationship with Jesus Christ, we were not brought up going to church every Sunday. It's good to know that God has a ram in the bush. Actually, for us, there were two rams in the bush: our grandmother and Aunt Dot. They were very religious ladies who exhibited many good morals and values. Although Black people lived together in their own communities, the only thing that would separate us from each other was religion. Neither our grandmother nor Aunt Dot would go to places or events where people would be drinking or carrying on in any other manner that they may have deemed unholy. People respected God a lot differently than they do now. Grandma and Aunt Dot most definitely loved God, and you could tell it by the way they lived, not just by the words that they said.

Differences in religion were not the only things that separated Blacks during that time. As time progressed, my father moved the family from West Tampa to Citrus Park, Florida, a rural town that was about 40 miles away. Life was quite different for us in Citrus Park, compared to what we experienced in West Tampa. For example, in West Tampa, we lived in a community of Black neighborhoods. In those times, segregation was legal, so Black people were forced to live in segregated communities.

Some people viewed segregation as a negative thing. Like anything else, it had its pros and cons. From what we experienced, though, segregation was not such a bad thing. I know that may have thrown you a bit, so let me explain. There was cohesion within our segregated communities. Everybody knew everybody. My friends' parents knew our parents, and we shared so many common things. Accordingly, Blacks were united. There was a stronger sense of identity among Black people, and we knew who our enemies were because racism wasn't something that was swept under the mat; it was out front. Particularly, Black adults had no ambivalence about how White people felt and how they would be treated if they went outside of their community and neighborhood.

Our parents understood this, so they kept us away from those negative influences. We had everything we needed. It was a duplicated society wherein Whites had their own schools, social events, etc. We had our own, too. All the teachers and students in our community were Black. We had Black-owned businesses. As a young person living in Tampa, I never had to engage or encounter White people or White institutions wherein there was an altercation. I'm sure this was a result of segregation. However, our reality was met with a rude awakening when we moved to Citrus Park because we were the first ones to integrate our elementary school.

This was a major transition because integration had just begun. As such, there was a lot of tension between the Black and White schools. When LaGrant was transitioning from the 6th to 7th grade, we had somewhat gotten settled in our new environment. Yet, I still knew my brother missed me from being with him while in school. He knew I would protect him from any bullying or any encounters with racism he may have had to face. By then, I was already in high school. Eventually, I ended up quitting school, fathering a child at a young age, and trying to find my way in life. While this was happening with me, integration still proved to be challenging for my little brother. Every day when he went to junior high school, there would be White boys waiting on him. In order for him to fend his way, he had to pretend he was crazy.

I had challenges, too, but most of mine revolved around me having a girl's name. I was teased quite a bit about my name. It got to a point that I'd end up getting into fights because of it. This bothered me to the point of not wanting to name my son after me. It was for this reason that I named my first son Telley. As I got older and more mature, I asked God to give me one more chance. He did, and the result is me having a second son named Shelley IV.

Nevertheless, back to what we experienced with integration and segregation. We used to travel to Inverness, Florida in the summertime by way of the Greyhound bus. When the bus stopped, we had to go to the "Blacks Only" section if we needed to go to the bathroom or if we wanted a drink of water. That was both puzzling and humiliating. Our parents tried to explain this to us, but it still made no sense to us and it most certainly did not seem fair. My mother, at times, would dress me like a king and tell me I was born to be a king. "Why would a king have to live like this," I would wonder. At the time, I just didn't understand.

When we moved to Citrus Park, I remember visiting a restaurant in a place called The Village. They were widely known for having big, delicious hamburgers. However, if we wanted to buy one, we had to go to the back door and place our order. LaGrant, who was ever-inquisitive, would look in the front of the restaurant and see people sitting down with their families. He couldn't help but wonder why

5

we couldn't do the same. One day, he gathered enough audacity to say, "I'm going to go in here, sit at the counter, and place an order. I'm going to see what they're gonna do. I'm just a little kid. What could they possibly do to me?"

Well, I have to tell you that my little brother was awfully bold. When he walked in there and sat down, the people looked at him like he was an alien. The waitress told him he had to go to the back door to place his order. He didn't want to make a fuss, so he complied. He was young, but he had enough sense to know that he didn't want any repercussions.

More specifically, he didn't want to face the possibility of having White people to come and start messing with us. That would be the normal consequence when Blacks went against the grain and started crossing the line of going into White folks' territory. It was very important that we stayed in our place, so to speak.

Not too long after that, we started getting visitors at night. MuhDear woke up in the wee hours of the morning; it had to be about around 1:00 or 2:00. The lights were out on the street. It was pitch black dark, but we noticed that there was a parked car in front of the house. MuhDear gave me a knife to help defend us should we need to protect ourselves. (My father wasn't there, so with me being the oldest, I had to be the man of the house.)

We ended up staying up all night watching and waiting. I was on one end of the house while she was on the other end. It was not a good feeling knowing someone was outside of the house. Anything could have happened; we had heard and seen situations before. After the eerie presence became unbearable, MuhDear ran down the street to a preacher's house for help. He came back with her and the car left.

It wasn't unusual for Black people to be placed in such a position of discomfort. Whites would come at different times of the night and park their cars on dirt roads. We had gotten accustomed to always being on the lookout, so we would see them, even if it was dark. One particular night, MuhDear, LaGrant and I had a friend of the family with us. He dropped us off and out of nowhere, a group of men tried to harass us. We knew it was the Ku Klux Klan.

Another instance of harassment and racism occurred when we were out on a lake. There was an old White lady who used to rent boats to us so that we could fish and swim. (MuhDear loved to fish as well as swim.) One day, LaGrant, MuhDear and I were in the middle of the lake fishing. When all of a sudden, a motorboat came speeding toward us. We were in a little paddleboat. They screamed, "You niggas get out of here." I thought they were going to turn us over. As we pulled up to dry land so we could get back to our car, the man who was driving the boat pulled up in a truck and told the old White lady, "If you rent some more boats to some more niggas, we're gonna burn your house down."

Needless to say, this was terrifying. Yet, I managed to remember the name that was printed on the truck. I said to myself, "When I get big, I'm going to come back and find him." It was those types of disheartening things that my family and I had to face in the early days. Those were hard times, to say the least. But it was that kind of mentality that caused Black people to support each other's businesses. We knew how White people thought and how they would do. They didn't put up any fronts about how they felt and what they would do. With that being the case, we knew we would need to do everything legally possible to grow and support our own endeavors. Knowing that my mother and father had the potential to put their individual abilities together and create something special, the time would soon come for the family business to begin.

Chapter 2

The Legacy Begins

Inequities among people of color is not an uncommon phenomenon. Black people in particular have always had to work harder and prove themselves to be just as good, if not better, than others. I learned this firsthand by growing up in the 1950s and 60s. As a result, I grew up knowing that succeeding in life wasn't optional. We had no choice if we wanted to experience a life embodied by any measure of substance.

My father and mother knew this all too well. My father knew what it meant to be the provider for his family. He had no problem working to take care of us. And it didn't take him long to discover that he would have to own his own success. He quickly realized that working a job for someone else would only prove to live up to the joke that says a job will keep you **Just Over Broke**. The common thought is that you'll make money, but the likelihood of being paid enough to see your own way would be slim. They'll pay you enough to keep you coming back for your next pay check.

While the concept of entrepreneurship is something that is admirable and desired by many, it should be understood that it is not something that every person is cut out for; everybody is not meant to be an entrepreneur. The word in Hebrew means "man of faith" and "risk taker." If you are not willing to take many risks and believe God at the same time, I suggest you think twice before going into business for yourself.

Being that my father understood how difficult things could be in terms of making a living for himself by working for someone else, he was willing to take risks and try his hand at entrepreneurship. He got his first glimpse at it when his father owned a restaurant in the 1920s or 30s in Camilla, Georgia. Perhaps this was part of what inspired him to believe he could run his own business as well. The idea picked up more steam when my father worked at a country club in Tampa. The owner, who was a White man, had a son who had gone to school to be an architect. During general conversations between my parents, the topic of my family members' excellent cooking skills would continuously come up. After many conversations, my mom had an idea of building a round, stainless steel diner. This was a brilliant idea because no one had done it before.

My mom articulated what she had in mind to the young architect. He, in turn, put her thoughts onto paper as a blueprint. She successfully obtained a permit from the City of Tampa to have the building built. First, they had to raise enough money, and then get a permit. After they combined their ideas, finances, and logistics for labor, the building was constructed. The rest is, as they say, history! Who would have ever thought that a restaurant model that has been duplicated by many was conceptualized by my mother? To me, that is beyond amazing.

So, the year was 1951. Anthony's Drive-Inn was born. Starting from very humble beginnings, I doubt if my parents had any idea whatsoever that their establishment would become a staple in the community. One of the things they sold every day was chili; it was one of their signature items. They also sold hamburgers, sweet potato pies and apple pies. Peach cobbler was a real treat as well. Sealtest ice cream, milkshakes, pie a la modes and Coke floats were among the other big hits. Because we were a 24-hour establishment, breakfast was a highly anticipated feature. Many truckers would stop by and get our signature corned beef, eggs, grits, and a cup of coffee before they would begin their day. It was our pleasure to serve them. It's amazing to think that a cup of coffee was $.11 back then! Meals would cap off at $4, regardless of what kind of meat was ordered.

As time progressed, soul food items like beef stew, baked and fried chicken, chitterlings, collard greens, baked beans, yellow rice, and many others became part of the menu. The bottom line of it all was that people knew they could come to Anthony's Drive-Inn and get a good meal along with professional and dignified service. The atmosphere was such that it provided a place for people to not only eat, but also have a good conversation about politics, religion, or simply the current events of the day. What a winning combination.

Being able to offer our customers a good product of excellent food and service has always been our standard. My mother and Aunt Sweetie were both good cooks, and they poured their heart and soul into the preparation of every item. I also remember how the staff took pride in what they did. It makes sense that they did because, as I stated earlier, I grew up in an era where Black folks had to do their best.

Accordingly, my parents made certain to keep me and my brother away from negative influences. We lived in a separated society: just as Whites had their own schools, social events, etc., so did Blacks. All of our teachers and students were Black. We had Black-owned businesses. Growing up in a segregated society created a great sense of identity amongst people in the community. All over the Tampa Bay area, there were several Black neighborhoods that represented a mixture of people. Lower class, middle class, and upper class all lived within the boundaries of a segregated society. This included doctors, lawyers, businessmen, teachers, and general laborers. We could walk down the street and pass the public housing community, which mostly housed the uneducated and the poor at that time. However, if we went 1,000 yards further in the community, we would see nice homes where Black professionals lived. This diverse mixture of classes of people from different educational and economic levels gave Black children the opportunity to see a vast array of role models.

Not only did we get to see role models in our community, but it was also important for MuhDear to affirm us and let us know that we were "somebody." I'll never forget how she would dress me up like a king. This is something that has had such a profound impact on me that I have chosen to pass the same process on to my sons and grandsons. I want them to know that they are kings. With the highest level of humility that I can share, I want them to know that they were born to be kings. I want them to know that when they give their life to God, that makes them part of royalty. It is up to them to accept it, embrace it, and walk in it.

The experiences of seeing Black role models in our community and being raised to believe that we (Blacks) were like kings instilled a great sense of pride within us as a people. For example, Black teachers were proud of their certification, and went to great lengths to assure that their education did not stop at the Bachelor's degree level. This explains why most of the Black teachers in the high schools (Blake and Middleton) had Master's and Ph.D. degrees. And if they didn't have advanced degrees, they were on their way to getting them. Remember, this was a time when Blacks always had to remain a step ahead. In most cases, it's still that way today.

The Black workers at the restaurant were a brilliant example of this. Take my Aunt Dot, for example. She worked there as a cashier and a waitress. She has told me many times how professional they were. They were neat in their appearance. Nobody came to work out of uniform. For the ladies, a full uniform consisted of not just their dress/skirt and blouse, but they also wore stockings, white shoes, a white cap, and an apron. Everything was pressed to perfection. They looked so well that they gave more of an impression like they were going to an event rather than to work. It didn't matter what kind of work they were doing. They weren't caught up in titles or big I's and little you's. They had a job to do, and they felt that regardless of the nature of the assignment, it was their task to be their best in every way.

Plus, they were working in a top-notch establishment. Anthony's Drive-Inn was not some juke joint. It was a real, 24/7 restaurant that folks came to by choice. There were other options, but our establishment was the standout in Tampa. If no one else could be counted on to give us their best, we at least owed it to ourselves to do so for ourselves and for one another. I am honored and humbled to say that this is what my parents did. It is heartwarming to hear people who can remember Anthony's Drive-Inn say that there still is no place in Tampa that gave the community what my family gave in terms of excellence in dining. To me, that speaks volumes to my parents' commitment.

In addition to MuhDear and Aunt Sweetie, other members of the family helped in the restaurant also. I have another cousin, Herman King, who is now well into his 70s who was a part of the early beginnings as well. He started working at the restaurant somewhere around 1956. Herman was the first member to attend and graduate college. He is a Morehouse College graduate.

The family dynamic of the business was very real and very special. It meant a lot to know that we could come together and operate on one accord. The concept of family's feuding, especially in the workplace is something that my family was blessed to avoid, according to my Aunt Dot. This is something she revealed to me and my sons in recent times during a visit to Tampa. She talked about how my father instilled family values of loving one another and working in unity. She also talked about how the women were not expected to work the graveyard shifts. This was a way of showing them honor and respect. Some of my cousins worked at the restaurant after school (and sometimes during the summer), and it made them feel good to know that they could make their own money and do something for themselves.

Outside of the family, one of the cooks was a Hispanic man by the name of Big Bobby. One of his specialties was deviled crabs. He also cooked soul food so very well that he was probably one of the better cooks out of the entire staff. A visit with Aunt Dot and my cousins also revealed that one of the things that set our restaurant apart was the fact that we had such great cooks. In addition to Big Bobby, there was Diretha, Johnnie Mae, and Mr. Turner. Each of them brought something special to the business. They also talked about how we took the time to lay the silverware out on the napkin – knife, fork, and then the spoon – fold it over and twirl it. We also had paper boxes as carry out containers. My father, whom they called Uncle Buddy, would make sure we folded the boxes early so that when the next shift came, they would not have to be slowed down by trying to make certain there were enough that were already prepared. My aunt and cousins also shared how my father was a stickler for order. He made sure money was always placed in the cash register properly. It was unacceptable to have bills folded, wrinkled, facing different ways, etc. If he saw that, he would make sure it was immediately corrected. My family and I chuckled when we talked about that because they already know that I will address this issue if I ever see it.

When Anthony's Drive-Inn first opened its doors, it opened on the corner of Main and Oregon. The building's design was that of the stainless-steel facility that was conceptualized by MuhDear. The business did very well for a long time, but some years later, the City came along and bought us out. It was then that we moved about three or four blocks down on Main Street to the heart of West Tampa and re-established the business in a business district of West Tampa. Along that business district, you had a plethora of Black-owned businesses. To the left of us was a print shop, which is where my dad got all his printing done. To the left of the print shop was a grocery store. There was a bar across the street called the Zanzibar.

Next to Zanzibar was the BBQ King, which happens to still be there and operational as of the writing of this book. On the other side of the Zanzibar was Bexley's Pool Hall. (During a recent visit, I had the opportunity to speak with the cook – the same cook that's still there worked for the original owner. This same person worked for the owner's daughter, and now he is working for the granddaughter.) As I got older, I found myself spending a lot of time at Bexley's; it was more time than I needed it to be. As a frequent visitor, I remember a game of pool costing 10 cents. People would come in there and play the numbers; so did I.

The business establishments were plenty in number; there were more. Across from dad's place was a dentist, Mr. Wright, which is where we got all our dental work done. Ralph's Shoe Shop was also located in the immediate vicinity. Mr. Ralph did everybody's shoes all over town. Black people spent their money with each other, and that was a beautiful thing.

Our restaurant grew steadily over the years. Before the City's buyout and our relocation to the corner of Main Street and Oregon, we lived behind the restaurant. After the buyout, though, my daddy built a house for us in the country; it was a small town called Citrus Park.

By this time, I believe I may have been in the 8th grade. I was at an easily impressionable age, and I could not help but take notice of how things were for Black people and how we had to act accordingly. The emergence of so many Black-owned businesses puts me in the mind of Atlanta, Georgia's historic Auburn Avenue. There are many accounts of its positive experiences during its time of flourishing. Black people were forced by law to practice Black empowerment. In other words, we had to empower ourselves because we were the only ones we could truly count on to do so. Some people may have perceived this as something negative. In essence, a generalized thought was that Black people didn't want to live as integrated Negroes alongside White people. The inferred implication was that Blacks preferred to live segregated.

Ironically, this is something Whites and people of other races still do today; it just has different names attached to it. Back in the day, it was identified by communities called Germantown or Chinatown. Nobody said anything negative about it because other races did not have, as Blacks did, the history of segregation laws to keep them out of the mainstream communities. In other words, they weren't forced to live in a segregated society like we were. However, if a Black person lived that way, it was viewed negatively. The fact remains that legalized segregation forced us to do what Whites and others were doing then and continue to do today. Whether we knew it or not, this forced us to develop our own businesses and support them. Without this sanction, Blacks wouldn't have experienced this kind of success. What it did was force Blacks to support each other.

Some believed that integration was created to work against us. Particularly, Dr. Martin Luther King Jr. was often accused of wanting to destroy our neighborhoods, which just wasn't true. What he did want to do was stop the disrespect we were receiving. It could not be denied that the Black restaurants had better food. Neither could it be denied that Blacks in our communities lived well. We had better education and we had skilled laborers. The missing link was that we didn't have all the necessary financial resources. And this is where the disrespect came in.

Furthermore, Blacks were taught to believe we were inferior. That's why a lot of Black teachers tried harder for a better education so no one would say they were second class. This climate that had been birthed caused Black people to think we were missing out on something. We thought everything about the Whites was better since they had new schools, material wealth, and other things that Blacks just did not have. Such harsh realities helped contribute to the concept of us being "the underdog" because it was crystal clear that the system was not designed to help Blacks.

The sting of these realities was taken to heart by my father. They caused him to understand clearly that he would, by all means, have to do his absolute best to not only survive but also thrive. He knew what he was doing because he was smart enough to start his business in the Black community. I shall forever be grateful for his tenacity as well as his foresight to "keep on keeping on" in a day and age when the odds were most definitely against him. The legacy had begun. The least I could do was try my hand at making sure the legacy and dream would live on.

Chapter 3

No Seconds for Me...I'm Not Hungry

There comes a time in every person's life when they want to find their own place in the world. This is particularly true if they have lived in an environment where a foundation has already been laid. In such instances, there is an expectation for them to follow in the footsteps of someone else. I experienced this for myself, but it wasn't a bad thing. My parents had done such a good job of owning and operating Anthony's Drive-Inn. Such a reputation was built that many people knew about us. They had found within our establishment a safe haven and a place for excellent food, service, and conversation. It was our delight to serve the people, so we took great pride in all that we did. Things were really going well.

By being a part of and watching the day to day operations of the restaurant, it was clear to me that my father was proud to have his family working together to make dreams come true. Every day presented an opportunity to establish the family's legacy further. While I realize this now, I must say that it did not have the same impact for me at 17- or 18-years old that it does today. We grow older and wiser as time progresses. In the process, we learn to see things from a much different perspective.

At that time, I was proud of what my family was doing. But, like any curious young person, I wanted to be able to stand on my own and do something that I could truly say I had done myself; it needed to be something I had done without the help of my family. As a young father, I really felt the need to prove that I could be "my own man" and take care of my family. One of the examples of manhood that I had seen within my father was that a man has his own, and he uses his own to take care of his family. This is exactly what I felt like I needed to do.

I also strongly believe that we succeed on the backs of those before us. As such, I further believe that it is our charge and our responsibility to succeed at a level greater than our forefathers. We have chances of doing something more than they were able to do. I watched my daddy be faithful to that which he had been entrusted. He worked so hard just to try to get more established. He was working so diligently just so he could provide a foundation for his family. By the time my brother and I came along, he tried to pour into us so that we could have a better life. And as we would go forth, we would be succeeding on the backs of those before us. That's something we can never forget. We must try to pay that forward.

So, the newborn desire that I had of doing some things on my own was not meant to minimize my father and all the hard work he had put into making the family business a success. No, not at all. This was simply something I felt an unwavering desire to do. I knew that whatever I ended up with, my ultimate goal would be to make my father and the family proud. This, I felt, would be a perfect way to pay it forward. With this goal in mind, I found myself going to search for work outside of the restaurant. One day I ended up at the Tampa Theatre building. I was fortunate enough to get a job delivering eyewear for an optical lab. This type of work was totally different from what I had become accustomed to from my work experience at the restaurant. However, I was persuasive and enthusiastic enough to be offered a job. The owners of the company were Steve and Patty Reid. Mr. Reid had another job as a truck driver for National Linen. Mrs. Reid had a working relationship with the eye doctors. They had a very nice operation set up.

I accepted the job with an attitude of gratitude and with a wealth of enthusiasm. I had finally accomplished something on my own. I now had achieved something that I pursued; no one gave it to me. The real truth of the matter was that it was the favor of God, whether I recognized it then or not. As I later learned what God's favor was all about, I also learned that it is something you cannot work for or earn. Yes, I worked and earned my wages at the restaurant. But that could not override my heart's desire to go out and speak for myself to the point of convincing someone who would not be partial to me (as family would) and give me an opportunity to prove that I could bring value to their enterprise. I did that, and it worked! That was an exhilarating feeling. It made me feel like I could stand on my own and take care of my family outside of the "ark of safety" that I was so used to.

This desire of mine may seem to be overrated by some. I realize there are some who may have felt like I had it made because of what had been established by my parents. I share how I felt at the time because I think it needs to be understood that sometimes when things are handed to us or made so easy for us to obtain, the very ones who were seeking to help us actually end up handicapping us. Most times that is not their intention.

Unfortunately, though, that's how it ends up happening. As a parent, what I have experienced is that some children will have a greater appreciation for things if they work for them themselves rather than expect things to be handed to them on a silver platter. When they don't work to earn the things they desire, it creates an opportunity for them to adopt a sense of entitlement. As a result, they can easily end up being rather ungrateful, and they will not take care of the things they accumulate as well as they would have if they had worked for them.

The more I think about it, I also realize that adults can be this way as well. Sometimes, different family situations may arise, causing a child to feel like they have missed out on some things during their childhood. As time progresses, the parents may have a better outlook or position in life. That child, who is now an adult, may look at the current situation and see it as a time to say things like, "Where's mine? That didn't happen for me. Why didn't things happen that way for me? Maybe you don't owe me, but you did more for them (the other children) than you did

19

for me." In my humble opinion, all I can say is that such things should not be. Regardless of the unpredictable outcomes, that doesn't mean that a parent cares more for one child than the other. The now-grown child should realize that situations can easily change a person's ability to provide. Perhaps the parents' situation did get better over a period of time. After all, the Bible does speak of your latter days being greater than your beginning. Of course, there will be times of struggle and uncertainty, but the key is to keep moving. Things will eventually get better. I do believe something is not right if your latter is not greater. After all the tests and trials, you should be wiser, and you should have learned to make better decisions.

Nevertheless, as a child or even as an adult, I knew I didn't want to have such feelings of entitlement. I wanted to stand on my own two feet and make my own money outside of the family's business. At the same time, I still wanted the same love and fellowship with my family that I always had. There was no need for love to be lost; and there wasn't. Of course, my decision to do something different wasn't something that my father was overjoyed about at the time. His natural desire was for me to remain with the family's business. Yet, he loved me enough to still to allow me to pursue my own endeavors.

That's why I always give my kids the opportunity to choose whether or not they want to be in the family business. Once I went into business for myself (still upholding the family's name), my kids had to work there at an early age in order to learn a work ethic. Not only did they gain a work ethic, but they also came to an understanding that nothing in life is free. When they got 18 and out of school, they could make their own decision of whether they would join the family business or move on. Regardless of the decision they made, it was still important that I supported them and gave them the opportunity to choose.

Another reason I needed to do something on my own was because of the struggle I had with gambling. As a teenager, I was a compulsive gambler. It later proved to be one of my downfalls. However, after having quit high school and after having become a teen father and husband, I found myself constantly hustling to take care of my family. It was unfortunate, but the ugly truth of the matter is that I was sucked into that lifestyle. The nearby pool hall and the money I earned from working at the restaurant made it easy for me to get caught up.

Also, you may have heard of people having addictive personalities. You may have also heard of generational commonalities; some people call them generational curses. Well, one thing I discovered about the Anthony men is that we are compulsive. If we find something that consumes us, we will become compulsive at it. And if you don't steer the compulsion in the right direction, it will destroy you. I saw that happen with different ones in my family. I saw the possibility of it happening to me, and I didn't want to face it.

Another way in which I saw the possibility of detriment was through some of my father's other work experiences. He was, at one time, part owner of a night club. It was a very popular place that hosted James Brown, as well as other Black entertainers who came through Tampa to jumpstart their careers in the entertainment industry. Although I was too young to get into the club at the time, my older cousin, Herman King, told me about the things that happened in the club. But I do remember seeing for myself a helicopter letting James Brown out at Tampa's Lopez Field so that he could make his grand entrance by sliding across the floor.

I also had the influence of a group of Black businessmen who had informally organized themselves as some kind of brotherhood; it seemed like they had an alliance of some sort because they had their own way of doing things. At any rate, there were several of them, and they would go to each other's houses and play poker. It was nothing for them to gamble on the weekends from Friday until Sunday night. They would also play poker at our house, and that was one of the ways I picked up gambling. Seeing them gamble regularly and with such ease made me think it was okay. I saw it all: everything from gambling to womanizing to drinking. I have learned that these things are first cousins to one another because they are sinful in nature. Now that I am a mature Christian, I thoroughly understand the need for adults to be careful about what we do and how we live. Every action is being taken in by our children, and whether we know it or not, we are setting examples for future generations.

For example, a boy may think the adverse actions that he witnesses of his parents are cool. However, what he is witnessing could easily impair him greatly if he chooses that same path as part of his life's direction. I'm thankful for having gained this knowledge as an adult. As a young man, I didn't know that; those things didn't seem to be problematic at the time. From my perspective, they were simply harmless things that men did. Remember, although I had godly examples through the persons of my grandmother, my Aunt Dot, my Aunt Aretha (Herman King's mother, whom we would see in the summertime when we went to Inverness...we used to call her Mama because she helped raise her sisters after her mother died), I was not brought up in the church. The principles of righteous living were not regularly shown to me. That is why it is so very important for a man to be a godly example.

I later realized what I had experienced was not right. And since I didn't want to follow suit, I knew I would have to seek a different path for my life. A change of environment, I believed, would do me a world of good. I believe God must have heard the desires of my heart and opened the door for me to start working at the optical lab. After I started working there, I began to create a reputation for being a good and dependable worker. I came to work every day and I was on time. Each day I availed myself to be open to whatever may present itself to me. There came a day when some of the guys who worked in the lab didn't show up for work. This is one time I saw for myself the relevance of the statements that say, "The show must go on," and, "One monkey don't stop no show." Whether they came to work or not, there was still work that had to get done. This opened the door for me to have more responsibility.

When Mr. Reid realized he was shorthanded, he called on me to help him in the lab. I did not hesitate. Sure, I could have been bashful. I could have told him I had never done anything like that before. He did not ask me if I had or not, so I did not feel the need to tell him anything different. I'm glad that I had a teachable spirit because it paid off for me at that time. It is amazing what you can learn when you have a mind that is open to receiving new ideas.

As I began to follow Mr. Reid's instruction and embrace my new duties for the day, one of the tasks I was given was that of helping to finish the lenses. In so doing, it was discovered that I had a knack for working with my hands. This one opportunity opened the door for me to work in the lab on a regular basis. As a result, I realized that I was doing something meaningful. "Hey! I'm working and helping to make people see better." That was a real "wow" moment for me. It is a heart-warming feeling to be able to do something that will benefit someone else. I was doing that, and I was doing it on a job that I applied for and was accepted into all on my own. In my mind, I had really achieved something big for myself. I had to pat myself on the back for that.

From that day on, every day became a day to learn more. The Reids were pleased with my abilities, and Mr. Reid made certain to teach me everything he could. Now that I think about it, I was really being blessed. I was being given firsthand knowledge in an industry in which I had no formal training. God placed me in a position to be taught by a professional. Back then, Black men couldn't take the State Board so they could become opticians. Therefore, I was getting an education without having to pay the financial cost. Yes, indeed, that was a blessing.

Every day I opened my heart and mind to take in all the knowledge and wisdom that Mr. and Mrs. Reid would pour in to me. Every day was a day to learn something different, to try harder, and to do better. I committed myself to doing just that. I was enjoying what I was doing and it was evident that they were still enjoying having me as a part of the team; I was just operating in a different capacity. As a fast learner, I caught on to everything I was being shown. That was a good thing because, over time, I was entrusted with running the lab.

That was a major milestone for me. There I was: a young father with a limited education running an optical lab. I was focused and determined, so there was nothing I could not do. I committed myself to doing the best job I could, so I approached each day with a winning attitude. The work that I did was commendable enough for me to be in on a transaction wherein the Reids sold a portion of the business to a businessman from Jacksonville. Little did either of us know that an even bigger transaction was waiting in the winds. A major change was on the way.

Chapter 4

Goodbye, Tampa! Hello, Atlanta!

Things were going well at the optical company, even with the owners having sold a portion of the business to a businessman from Jacksonville. As the business continued to progress, it caught the attention of the biggest optical company in the world, Milroy Optical. They were so impressed that they came in and bought out the whole company. This was about a couple of years or so after I had begun working with the Reids.

With the buyout came the opportunity for a lab to be opened in the Atlanta (Georgia) area. Guess who the Reids trusted with a part of this major responsibility? Me, of course! What an opportunity this would be, I thought. I visited Atlanta and stayed for about a week. The purpose of the trip was for me to get a feel for the area and see if it would be someplace I would like to relocate. From all indications, Atlanta would be a great place for me to live. Even though I thought moving to Atlanta was a good idea, it still meant that I would have to face my father and inform him of my decision.

I knew he would be disappointed because of his desire to have me stay home and help with the family business. As I suspected, he didn't want to let me go, *but he did and he also gave me his blessings. He gave me his last $1,000 and told me to go and make the family proud.*

I didn't realize it then, but the combination of my father's blessing and the move itself was actually God's doing. Just like earlier blessings I received that I didn't quite understand or truly know if I deserved, this opportunity was also an example of the favor of God, which He had so kindly decided to bestow upon me. I now plainly see it as a move of God because He was taking me out of an environment that would only be to my great detriment if I did not find a way of escape. And that way of escape was the move to Atlanta.

I mentioned in the previous chapter that I was a teen father and husband, but I didn't share the details of how this came to be. As I divulge now, the detriment that I just referenced will make more sense. I worked in my father's restaurant as a teenager. It was a well-put-together establishment that, admirably, had rooms in the upstairs area that stood over the restaurant. Because there was a need to spend large increments of time there (since it was a 24-hour facility), I had a room myself. And because I was there quite often, I got a chance to see the teenagers that wanted part-time jobs during the school year or in the summertime. My daddy understood this, and he would hire students.

Naturally, the chemistry, the curiosity, and the temptation that present themselves when teens are around each other found its way to me. As a result, I impregnated a girl. This was not the plan that I had for myself. It wasn't the plan my parents had in mind either. Yet, it was my reality. It was a reality that I had to face as well as embrace. I would soon be the father of a beautiful baby girl. The question, then, became, "What in the world am I going to do?" My daddy wanted me to keep going to school. Hindsight is always 20/20 vision. I wish I had complied with my dad's wishes, but I quit school in the 10th grade and got a job. The respectable thing to do was to get married, and that is what I did.

Even with working, the rude awakening was that the wages I was earning just was not enough for me to take care of my family. I knew that my daddy loved me. I knew, beyond the shadow of a doubt, that he would give me his last and do whatever he needed to do to help me. However, there was something on the inside of me that caused me not to want my daddy to have to take care of my family. After all, he was the one who had always instilled in me that a man takes care of his own. A man should not have to depend on anyone to do that for him. But how could I possibly do that on the meager wages that I was earning? I just knew that someway, somehow, there had to be a better way.

That better way for me was gambling. After I made that realization is when I started hustling in the poolroom. I had the influence of family members that I had seen gambling, and there was also an older guy that I knew who was a gambler. He couldn't drive a car, but he was a serious pool player and hustler. I would watch these guys play, and I would play as well. I would also play dominoes. What some may have perceived merely to be fun and games were actually the elements that contributed to me becoming a compulsive gambler. Even though I was working to make an honest living, I still found myself gambling. I just had to do it. When I would get off work at night, off to the pool hall or to play dominoes is where my feet would tread. Where ever the guys were is where I went.

I can agree with those who say that desperate people do desperate things. I was desperate and determined to take care of my family, but I was also desperate and determined to satisfy my gambling addiction. As such, there were some desperate measures that I found myself taking. One was that of taking money from the restaurant (before I moved to Atlanta.) I knew it was wrong, but at that time, being right was not my major concern. As my desperate measures remained unceasing, I decided I would give my best shot at the dog track. In my own way of thinking, I believed this would be an easy win for me because the dog that I would be betting on, LB's Dallas Girl, had been winning for me all year long.

Things were going well until I looked up at the monitor and saw that she (the dog) had gotten tangled and started flipping. "What in the world? This couldn't be happening," is what I thought to myself. I spent all I had. The worst part of it for me was that "all I had" was not my own. Remember, I had taken money from the restaurant. It had to be somewhere around $700-$800. Man, this was $700-$800 I knew

I could not replace. How would I explain this to my daddy? When I finally mustered up enough courage to tell him, he didn't appreciate what I had done at all. He was beyond livid.

Unfortunately, my gambling compulsion did not cease when I made my move to Atlanta. As a matter of fact, it only got worse. I found myself flying from Atlanta to Tampa on Fridays after work just so I could gamble. I would get a round-trip ticket so I would at least know I had a way back home. Now that I think about it, I was really bound by this addiction. I was so bound that I could not even think clearly. If I was thinking clearly, it seems to me (now) that I could have found a local pool hall to gamble in rather than waste money on a flight. What was I thinking? It's obvious that I wasn't thinking logically if I was even thinking at all. Granted, playing dominoes was a big deal in Tampa. Nevertheless, it still seems to me that I could have found another way rather than spending money on a flight.

I should also note that when I discovered my gambling addiction (when I was in my teens), I went to Gambler's Anonymous. I sincerely wanted to try to break the hold. Even with all the effort that was made, going to Gambler's Anonymous only slowed the addiction down. The "cure" I so earnestly wanted was not to be found; at least not then and not through that method of intervention.

As I take a retrospective look at this now, it just seems foolish. That is what happens when you allow your mind to be clouded with the things that are not meant to do you any good. I must say, however, that I did find a place or two to gamble in Atlanta, but the atmosphere simply was not the same as what I was used to in Tampa. You see, Atlanta didn't have the dog tracks and Jai Alai games. So, there was a major difference in what Atlanta had to offer in terms of gambling compared to what I knew and experienced back home. I couldn't get the feel of Atlanta's gambling scene. My addiction wasn't fed the same in Atlanta as it was in Tampa.

My excursions of flying to Tampa to gamble continued for about a year. I would gamble and lose all that I had. After a while, I just got tired of coming back home on Sunday broke and disgusted. I knew things would need to change for the better. My mind was forever wondering and wandering, and it got to a point where I found myself wanting to go back to my roots of the restaurant business. With that thought, I decided to open Butch's Slide Inn Bar-B-Q. I found a location on the borderline of Atlanta and Decatur, Georgia near the intersection of Candler and Glenwood Roads.

Surely, I thought, this would be an instant success. Why wouldn't it be? I had learned so much from my parents, I had skills of my own, and I knew what I was doing. To add to this, I had additional support from MuhDear, who would come back and forth to Atlanta to help me out. My father never did get a chance to come to Atlanta, but he knew I had opened a restaurant. Although he didn't get to see me in business, I know he would appreciate my decision to follow in his footsteps. The harsh reality, though, was that I wasn't really making any money with the business. The good thing was that I was making enough money on the job to support it. But even with that, it became clear to me that my bosses at the optical firm had somewhat of an attitude about me having a side business.

Still determined to do something positive and work in the best interest of my family, I purposed in my heart to do all I could to make Butch's Slide Inn Bar-B-Q a great success. When it was time to open Butch's Slide Inn, I took a week's vacation, beginning on a Friday. I remember the first day of business being on a Friday; we opened at 11 a.m. In addition to my signature bar-b-q and side items, I was selling beer. I was so excited that I stayed open until 4:00 Saturday morning. Yet, I was terribly disappointed to see that all I did was $150 worth of business. This had to be a joke! How did that happen? Knowing no other recourse, I found myself being mad at my mama and my daddy because I figured they didn't tell me something that I needed to know in order to make the business successful. They had to, because how could anybody live off $150 in sales?

Luckily for me, I was still working at the optical firm. I had a steady paycheck coming in from the job, plus I was still doing a little hustling.

As a young man, this was my system of survival. There is a lot that goes with being an entrepreneur in the restaurant business and being successful. As I mentioned before, entrepreneurship hinges greatly on risk-taking. Another major aspect is that of expenses. For example, on the surface, it may appear that the only expense a restaurant owner has to think about is purchasing food.

The truth is that there are so many more expenses to keep in mind. Workers have to be paid, supplies have to be purchased, considerations have to be made for marketing and advertising, there are utility costs, and the list goes on and on. Thus, there was always a possibility that you could have to pay more out than you would have coming in.

I would later recall the wisdom of my father and how he always used to tell me, "You've got two things you've got to control in the restaurant business if you want to survive and do well: that's food and labor. If you can handle those, you can make it. The restaurant business is a penny ante business; you've got to learn to count pennies in order to have dollars in the restaurant business. That's what the sales tax people (the government) understand, and you have to pay them every month." That's wisdom I learned along the way that I'll never forget and always appreciate.

Even with the frustration and disappointment from those early days, I was determined not to give up. At this point, I had stopped going back and forth to Tampa gambling. While I continued to give the business my all, I still found myself going back and forth to Florida because it was home and where my family was.

I always wanted to buy a car from where my dad bought cars for my mom. Between the restaurant and my job, I remember doing well enough to buy myself a brand-new Buick. The model of the Buick was known as a Deuce and a Quarter, and it was commonly referred to as "the Black man's Cadillac." It was important for me to let my family in Tampa know I was doing alright for myself. I remember my dad's words of encouragement for me to make the family proud. My new car gave me something to provide a tangible perception that I was doing well.

I appreciated the fact that I still had my job at the optical firm, but after a while, the owners began to feel like there was a conflict of interest. With that, I would have to make a decision, and I decided to go with the business. Seeing those low-sales days of $150 was disheartening, but I didn't want to give up. I tried everything I could to keep the business going, and I kept the momentum for as long as I could. A few years later, around 1979-80, I ended up selling the business. This was one of those painful decisions, but it was what I felt was best at the time.

The decision to sell the business was not the only tough decision that was made in my life. My first marriage saw its demise early on. After I moved to Atlanta, I married and divorced again. Each of the first two marriages produced a child, Consuelo Vanessa (Van) Anthony and Telley James Anthony, respectively. The gift of fatherhood is something that I am truly grateful for. It is true that we live and we learn. Despite the fact that I became a father at a young age did not take away from me learning about the importance of fatherhood. My life has been enriched by the lessons learned as well as by the opportunities God has given me to learn. He had enough patience with me to help me be a better person and a good father to my children.

Being able to be a good father is something I've always regarded as one of life's most important tasks. A man must do all that he knows how in order to raise his family in the ways of the Lord. Sure, people will try to advise you on what they think is best, but basically all a man can do is all he knows how to do. In fact, life has taught me that all you can do as a parent is what you know how to do. This is why you should get as much learning beforehand as possible. Sometimes, it's hard for a child to see that their parents are doing their best. Just as a child can grow into adulthood and feel a sense of entitlement when things get better over time, it's also easy for them to say there are favorites. My kids have said that of me, but I really do love them all the same. Each of them has their own personality traits; they are their own person, and I love and appreciate them for who they are.

I will talk about each of my children in greater detail later in the book, but for now I will provide a brief preview of my thoughts about them. I fathered my oldest daughter, Consuelo, when I was in high school. She has grown to be a wonderful mother and professional young lady. After moving to Atlanta and going through a divorce, I had my second child, Telley. I believe I shared earlier how I used to get picked at all the time by having a girl's name. I didn't want my firstborn son to have to go through the same thing I went through, so this is why I named him Telley. As I got older, I started to realize the importance of keeping the name Shelley Anthony going. I was Shelley Anthony III. My granddaddy, whom I never knew, was named Shelley Anthony, which made my father Shelley II. Since I now understood the importance of keeping the family's name going, I asked God to give me one more chance so I could do that. Thus, my fifth child, who was born after my bride, Diane, and I got married is named Shelley IV.

You may have noticed that none of us Shelleys or Telleys have juniors or seniors attached to our names. I like to believe that kings, which I was raised to believe I had the likeness of, are not juniors and seniors. Rather, we are IIs, IIIs, IVs, etc. This is why you see such attachments to our surnames. We were born to be kings, and the way in which we identify ourselves by way of our names only solidifies our belief. Our other children are Nina Marie Anthony; then Tina Denise Anthony, and Angel Lydia Anthony. Again, I will share more insight on our children a little later in the book.

I have shared with you the blessing of my children, but I would be remiss if I didn't also share with you how God smiled on me in 1981. It was at that time God blessed me with my rib, my soul mate, my best friend, my wife, Diane. Indeed, she is the "good thing" that I believe has brought favor in my life. This is what the Bible speaks of in Proverbs 18:22, "Whoso findeth a wife findeth a good thing, and obtaineth favour of the Lord." My relationship with her set the stage for a new chapter in my life to be written. At the time this book is being written, we have been together for 36 years, 34 of which we have been married. I know God has blessed me tremendously by allowing me to find her. For that, I shall forever be grateful.

Chapter 5

WHEN YOU HAVE "A GOOD THING," THE BAD THINGS AREN'T SO BAD

The year was 1981. I was 28-years old. At this point in my life, I knew I needed a wife. I knew I needed someone in my life who would love me unconditionally through the good and bad, the joys and pains, the ups and downs, the highs and lows.....through every conceivable contrast that life is sure to bring. For me, that someone was Barbara Diane (Johnson) Anthony, whom I simply and affectionately call Diane; I refer to her as my queen.

I remember the day I met her. It was the middle of the day, and I was sitting in the Pizza Hut on Candler Road (in Decatur, Georgia) having lunch. I saw Diane when she walked in, and I noticed how she seemed to appear a little fearful. It was almost as if she was tipping and wondering if anyone saw her come in. I thought that was strange, but even so, I could not help but notice how beautiful she was. She placed the order for her food and walked out of the restaurant. Before I knew it, I had gotten up out of my seat, walked out behind her, and asked for her phone number. She wouldn't give it to me, but she did allow me to give her mine.

Although I cannot say that I was truly saved at the time, I can say that I remember having prayed for God to send me a wife prior to the day I saw Diane at Pizza Hut. I had grown tired of living a life that kept me in uncommitted relationships. Some would call it fast living or street life. No matter the term associated with it, my reality was that I had no one that I could truly call my own that I felt I could spend the rest of my life with. That had become a major concern to me.

After all, I was a man. I was a man who was in need of true love. Secondly, I had two children, and I was totally committed to making sure that I played an active role in their lives. That would require some help; I knew I couldn't raise them on my own. I would do my best, but I still realized I needed support. I would especially need help if my business ventures would flourish as I had so earnestly hoped.

I remember praying and asking God to send me one woman that I could be satisfied with. I also asked Him to send me one that would help me raise my two children willingly, lovingly and unselfishly. Diane was the one. After a beautiful courtship, we got married July 28, 1983. It wasn't an elaborate ceremony, but it was filled with lots of love and happiness just the same. The only family member that was there was MuhDear. After we said our vows, I went back to work that evening. As simple as things were with us getting married, we were still overjoyed. That's how our marriage started but God said that our ending would be better than our beginning. Our blended union has been blessed by six children: Consuelo Vanessa Anthony, Telley James Anthony, Nina Marie Anthony, Tina Denise Anthony, Shelley Anthony IV, and Angel Lydia Anthony.

I shared in the previous chapter the Bible verse that references that when a man finds a wife he finds a good thing and obtains favor from the Lord. I believe what makes my wife a good thing is her relationship with God. I really feel like the Word of God is speaking of me in that verse; I must have been the one in mind when it was written! Of course, I know I'm not the only married man on earth. I just believe the Word of God in its entirety. I believe that as a Christian, I have the right to accept God's Word and apply it to my lifTherefore, when I read that a man's wife is his good thing and that she brings favor in his life, I believe that to be true for me.

There are many reasons why I believe this. For one thing, Diane has always been there for me. If I could create my own dictionary and define the word helpmate, I would simply place Diane's picture there. She was the helpmate God knew I needed. She was made just for me, and I was made just for her. She has made so many sacrifices for me, for our family and for the business.

A year or two before I met Diane, I made the decision to sell Butch's Slide Inn. However, I was still making the bar-b-q sauce for the new owners in my apartment, and I never let go of my entrepreneurial dreams. My desire to open another restaurant intensified even more after my father passed away. There would be many sacrifices that would have to take place in order to make this dream a reality, and I knew I had to have a strong, virtuous woman to help me. Consider this sacrifice, for example. There were times when I didn't have money to buy new dresses for Diane to wear to church. She didn't complain. Instead, she used her ability to sew and made her own dresses. I would sometimes get upset with myself because I couldn't provide for her the way I wanted to, but my wife would never make me feel bad. And if she felt bad about it, she never gave me any indication of it.

When we first got together, Diane didn't know anything about cooking or the restaurant business. I'm grateful that MuhDear took the time to come to Atlanta to help us out. I'm just as grateful that Diane was open to learning all she could from my mother. That's not always the case because we've all heard the old wives' tales that say, "You can't have two cooks in the kitchen," and, "There will always be problems when there are too many cooks in the kitchen." Given the possibility for catastrophe, based on those sayings, I truly appreciate the fact that my mother was willing to help Diane, and I appreciate the fact that Diane was willing to learn.

Another one of Diane's admirable qualities that I love is her love for God. In fact, it was her faith that attracted me to her all the more. She didn't just tell you she was a child of God; she lived it. You could tell it in the way she walked, in the way she talked, and how she treated people. All of these things were important to me. I believe it was her faith that helped see me through the difficult times of being an entrepreneur because being an entrepreneur is not an easy thing. Many people like the idea of working for themselves because of the flexibility it offers and because of the idea of calling their own shots. That's only a small part of it.

The real truth of it is that the risks that come along with entrepreneurship can be more overwhelming than many people can bear to stand. It can be especially challenging for men. You see, it doesn't look good for a man when Friday (payday) rolls around and he doesn't have any money. For a person who does not understand entrepreneurship, it could be very easy to adopt a negative attitude when money is not there. The attitude could be, "What do you mean you don't have any money? Haven't you been working all week?" Diane understood, and I know it was because God had endowed her with the Fruit of the Spirit, which includes compassion and patience.

These virtues have certainly been a blessing to me during my entrepreneurial journey. There are many things I've experienced and endured along the way that would have easily taken a person out or caused them to quit. In every situation, Diane was there to help me get through it. One such instance occurred during our courtship. We started construction on a building, but the contractor whom we entrusted with the job took our money without properly completing the job. It was a very terrible situation. It was so bad that there was little hope that we would overcome the way in which we had been cheated. But God had a plan. As time went on, we were finally able to get it done. The restaurant was open and we got married a few months after that.

Another instance occurred at a time when the business was six figures in the red. Diane knew it and she would just stay home and pray and pray and pray. She would even pray over the checkbook. She prayed that God would bring us out. One day, I woke up and the checkbook was out of the red. To this very day, I still don't know how God did it, but I know it was His doing. How grateful we were. We are still grateful today.

As I grew closer to my wife, her faith began to have an influence on my faith. She had been born and raised in the church, and the love she had for God caused me to want to know Him in a better way. The denomination to which she belonged was the Church of Christ. I remember being in church with her one Sunday. I listened intently to the preacher, but what he was saying didn't line up or match with what I had read for myself about the Holy Ghost. In my own way of desiring to know more about the things of God, I began to wonder about the infilling of the Holy Ghost. I later learned that, at that time, this was something that her church didn't believe in. Still, I remember reading in my Bible in Acts 2:4, "And they were all filled with the Holy Ghost, and began to speak with other tongues, as the Spirit gave them utterance." In other words, I wanted to know about people speaking in tongues.

Still extremely curious, I asked Diane about it, but she couldn't provide any insight. My curiosity did not end there. I asked the preacher about speaking in tongues and he told me, "It's not for today." I wasn't sure if he meant that it would not happen there on that particular day or if such did not happen during the present time. Either way it went, I still felt like something was not right because of what I had read for myself in my Bible.

I'm grateful that God has given me a level of spiritual maturity that now helps me to realize my reason for wanting to know about the infilling of the Holy Ghost. I believe it is because I would need its supernatural power to help sustain me. I would especially need it as I endeavored to build what God has now blessed to become an empire. Doors had begun to open for the business (which we called This Is It! Fish, Shrimp and More. We will talk more about the business in the next chapter.) There would be many mountains and hills to climb. There is no way that Diane and I would be able to overcome all that would come our way without the power of the Holy Ghost.

God remained faithful to us. As we were blessed, God continued to allow His grace and favor to shine upon us. We had seen some bad days, but I'm thankful that He gave me my "good thing." It is because of her that even the bad things weren't so bad. The journey had just begun. The path was now clear for us to start moving in God's plan and prepare ourselves to receive the full manifestation that was yet to come.

Chapter 6

Movin' on Up

In 1983, my beautiful bride, Diane and I, were still enjoying the blessings of marital bliss. She brought so much joy to my life, and it meant a lot to have that special someone whom I could share all my life's experiences with, whether they were good or bad. Even though I had stopped making the bar-b-q sauce for the people to whom I sold Butch's Slide Inn, the flame of the entrepreneur's spirit was something that I just could not seem to extinguish. In 1983, Diane and I took a leap of faith and began owning and operating This Is It! Fish, Shrimp and More. Today, we are known far and wide as This Is It! Bar-B-Q and Seafood.

Although the second part of the business' name changed, we have always remained true to This Is It! The name itself was inspired by the tagline created by Atlanta's signature brand, Coca-Cola. At the time, their slogan, "Coke Is It" was not only very popular, but it was catchy, too. To me, it only cemented in my psyche that, even though there are other options to quench one's thirst, Coca-Cola was the best choice. Naturally, this was a good move for Coke's executives. After all, with Coca-Cola's headquarters being in Atlanta, who wouldn't be drawn to this iconic brand? The chances of that happening were slim to none.

A lesson I had learned just from my own observations in business was to choose a name that would have a ring to it and make a strong statement at the same time. Sure, there are countless other restaurants people could have chosen to patronize. But our thought, from a marketing perspective, was that we had the best. So, there it was: This Is It!

As time went on, Diane and I experienced the many highs and lows of being entrepreneurs. One thing is for sure: it was not an easy ride; entrepreneurship never is, but at the end of the day, if it's God's plan for your life, it's worth it all. I recall coming home every day telling my wife the highlights of my day. She was always loving, supportive, and encouraging.

Our first location was at the intersection of Campbellton Road and DeLowe Drive in the Woolworth Shopping Center. It was a 2,500-square foot leased space. One of the things I remember about this location is that we had pool tables and that we didn't serve alcohol. The restaurant had a dining area, and we also had a walk-up window. There were several different businesses along the walkway, and our walk-up window was one of our main attractions. Our customers could order from the window or they could walk in and place their order. Our ability to fry the fish right there from the window was really something to see.

As the business continued to grow, it was important for me to see growth in my faith as well. I just had to get to know God in a better way. Yes, I was going to church on a regular basis, but I can't say that I was totally saved at the time; I wasn't wholeheartedly surrendered to God in every way. My walk with God got stronger, indeed, but I still was not at a point where I was filled with the Holy Ghost. We continued to go to church, and Diane was filled with the Holy Ghost in 1986. Finally, my breakthrough came in 1987: I received the infilling of the Holy Ghost! (You may recall me sharing earlier that I really and truly desired to be filled with the Holy Ghost and have the evidence of speaking in tongues.)

We will talk more about how I received the Holy Ghost in the next chapter. However, I needed to mention the fact that I did receive it. This is important because not long after I received the infilling of the Holy Ghost, I received a prophecy that God would bless us with another location. A mother at the church saw me riding around I-285 looking for a building so we could have a new location. For those who are not familiar with Atlanta, I-285 is the city's main interstate. Its route is circular, meaning that it goes in a complete circle; it can take you all over the metropolitan area repeatedly if you don't get off at your exit. We were pleased and honored that God was allowing us to do a considerable amount of business with our current location at the time, but I felt like the time had come for us to expand.

As I was searching for an additional site, I came across a Waffle House that was located at Washington Road and I-285. I asked the person who was in charge of Waffle House's real estate for a lease and some time to purchase the building. He complied by extending a 3-year lease, even though their ultimate goal was to sell the building. If I wanted to purchase the building at the end of the three years, I would need $150,000. Simply put, we would need to come up with the money to buy the building at the end of the 3-year period or move out. I saw us being entrusted with the 3-year lease as God's way of showing favor toward us. I trusted that He would work it out and make a way for us to be able to purchase the building when the time would come.

Well, that is exactly what God did! I was so thankful that Citizens Trust Bank loaned me the money to buy the building. This was the second piece of evidence I had that showed the benefits of having a good name and living right for God. (The first one came when God allowed me to purchase a brand-new Cadillac, which happened only two or three years prior to us purchasing the building. I will talk about that blessing shortly.) This was important because prior to the loan being approved, God was already dealing with me about the way in which he wanted me to do business with integrity.

Things went well for us at the Washington Road location, which we called This Is It! Seafood, but we would soon see a change. A shopping center was built across the street from us in 1987. Business dealings over the years had taught me that new competition always needs to be addressed. Therefore, I leased space in the shopping center and opened This Is It! Bar-B-Q. In order to address the competition, I made certain to go into a "no competition" agreement with the developer. This meant that the developers could not lease to another restaurant. So, there we were: This Is It! Seafood on one side of the street (in the former Waffle House) and This Is It! Bar-B-Q on the other side (in the new shopping center.)

Everything was going very well, and by 1989, we had begun looking for, found, and opened a new location in Decatur. It was no coincidence that a shopping center was being built at the intersection of Memorial Drive and Covington Highway. This would prove to be the ideal place to combine the concept of bar-b-q and seafood. Truly, God was enlarging our territory. From that point on, every establishment of ours would be called This Is It! Bar-B-Q and Seafood.

The good news of how well we were doing began to spread so fast that we started getting calls from other developers to expand our business in their areas. One such establishment was the West End Mall. This mall, along with the City of Atlanta, offered us money to build the space out. It sounded like a good idea. After all, what kind of sense would it make to turn down money, especially if it was going to help move our business forward?

The deal progressed, but when it was time to sign the lease, that quiet, still voice of God told me not to do it. Unfortunately, I ignored His voice and signed the lease anyway. In my mind, I didn't see it as the voice of the Lord. Instead, I looked at it as the devil trying to block our blessing. So, we went on and opened the restaurant anyway. We were doing well for about a year, but God already knew what was in the future for the West End Mall. When He told me not to sign the lease, He already knew that the main stores – Sears, Sunshine's, and Butler's – were going to close. The loss of these stores would ultimately have an impact on the number of customers coming into the mall. In turn, that would influence our business in a negative way; we would have fewer customers. That's why it's important to listen to that still, small voice. God knew, but I didn't.

God was trying to keep me from facing such a downturn. It seemed like the mall just went to the pits. I realized my error because the Lord had already warned me by telling me not to sign the lease. My decision caused us to be stuck in that particular location for approximately seven years. Yes, I was stuck. This was my largest investment, but I knew I couldn't walk away from it because of my promise to God about keeping my name right. I had told Him I would do everything within my power to do so. Walking away from that location would have caused me not to live up to the lease I had signed. In other words, it would cause me to jeopardize keeping my name right. Nevertheless, I knew I had to do something. Whatever I decided, it would have to be something that would allow me to maintain my integrity.

My final decision was to sell the business to someone in the mall. Even so, I still had to pay the monthly lease on the space and on the equipment. This was a financial challenge because banks and other financial institutions would not loan money to restaurants and night clubs. Their logic was that too many businesses of this kind go out of business rather quickly, usually within a year or two. Therefore, I was stuck with not only paying the lease, but also for the leasing of the equipment, of which the rates were exuberant. So, whether I kept operating the facility or not, I still had to pay for the lease of the equipment in order to keep my name and credit in good standing. Through it all, God kept reminding me of my name. "You have to keep your good name, Butch." I kept my vow to God, and no negative transactions from this deal ever showed up on my credit.

God showed me that He is the only one who knows the future. You have got to let Him lead. I learned this because after going through so many experiences, He showed me that when things are going good, it's hard to see and truly understand that they are actually good. This was a very serious lesson that I learned. Oddly, it's just as hard to go against what you think is good because the enemy will always come in and try to confuse your thoughts. God must always be your source. Even when you start thinking you can't make it, you must always remember that God is faithful, regardless of what the enemy may try to make you think. You should always pray and ask God to help cast out all negative thoughts from your mind.

The scenery of our business location on Washington Road began to change as time moved on. We had already experienced one change with the arrival of the shopping center across the street. We would soon learn that we would surely have to lean on God all the more. For example, when drug activity increased and eventually started taking over, we witnessed a decrease in patronage because no one wanted to feel unsafe. We also had a location in Greenbriar Mall, and things began to change there as well. Located on the south side of Atlanta in the Ben Hill community, this once highly frequented source of retail for many affluent African-Americans somehow transformed itself into a "tennis shoe mall." What was once a well-received place of choice for many customers had become a hangout spot that sold more sportswear instead of the niceties for which it was once popular. This, of course, had a negative impact on our business.

There were many struggles during those times as we tried to continually grow our business and keep our head above water. While we experienced some very painful times through the years, we also experienced some happy days and some marvelous experiences. We met some pretty incredible people along the way, too. One such person was James "Alley Pat" Patrick, who recently passed away (2015). Those who are from Atlanta will know him as a legendary, one of a kind guy. To some, he was known as the best friend of the late Rev. Hosea Williams. I simply called him my friend and mentor. He had a television and radio show, and we advertised the business with him. Somehow, he took a special liking to me and Diane.

After seeing us achieve a measure of success in business, he expressed to me his frustration of seeing supposedly well-to-do Negroes (he called us the "N" word) riding in raggedy cars. He thought that if we were doing well, we should at least have a decent car to show for it. That's when he decided to take me to Scrolls Cadillac. Knowing that I had filed for bankruptcy two or three years prior, I told him I couldn't buy a car. He paid me no attention and told me to come and go with him to the dealership so we could talk to the sales manager. I did, and the guy asked me how much I could afford to pay.

Knowing that I was not in the best of financial situations, I took a stroll out on the lot and fixed my eyes on a 1986 yellow Cadillac Sedan Deville. I went back in and told the sales manager what I thought I could afford. He told me to give him a few minutes. When he came back in he said to me, "Mr. Anthony, you can buy any car out here you want. You don't have to pay anything down and your payments will be lower than what you said you could pay." Keep in mind that I had only been saved 6-8 months. I was afraid to do something wrong. I didn't want to disappoint God and I knew He was watching, so I didn't accept the offer. I know there are many people who would have jumped on the offer without a second thought. Without any doubt, they would have called it a blessing from God and shouted all the way home. In the back of my mind, I thought because of Alley Pat's prominence, he had done something wrong, and I didn't want to be a part of it.

I will never forget Alley Pat's reaction when I told him what I had done. He cussed me out all the way back to Ben Hill. A week or so passed and I was still thinking about the car. It was a real beauty; I just couldn't get it out of my mind. After talking to Diane, we decided to go back to the dealership to see if the car was still there. When I returned to the dealership in a week, to my surprise, the car was still there. The sales manager was upset about the situation because other people had come by the dealership wanting to purchase the car for themselves. The problem was that, although I had completed the paperwork, I had not signed it. When I got back to the dealership, I was still contemplating. After I excused myself and went to the men's room, I heard a still, small voice say to me, "The car is yours." I felt a release that let me know it was okay to go back in and seal the deal.

It made sense to me because I read and understood for myself Proverbs 22:1, which says, "A good name is rather to be chosen than great riches, and loving favour rather than silver and gold." What I have discovered is that most people go after the fine silver and gold and forget about their name. With the few people that I counsel about business, I ask them, "How's your name?" It is important for me to instill in anyone who wants to do well in business to get their name right first and keep it right. When that happens, money will find you. Your name, according to the Bible, is more valuable than the money you're going after.

It was interesting to see how things unfolded. Diane drove the new car home, and I went back to work. When I got home later on that night, I told her I had heard the Lord say He went to the credit bureau and straightened out my name. This is how I was able to get approved for the car. Wow! God loved me enough to do that for me. What a mighty God I serve! I felt like I had no choice but to keep my name right because of my journey. This would be my way of showing my humility and gratitude to God for the many blessings He had bestowed upon my life. I made a promise to God that I would be faithful in keeping a good name, especially when it comes to bills, tithes, and offering. I shared this promise with my wife, and we both agreed to keep the promise.

God had done so many great things, and I knew greater things were to come. He had been with us from the very beginning, and there was no doubt that he had brought us from a mighty long way. Our business was progressing, and the best was still yet to come. Just seeing this and knowing this reminds me of Jeremiah 29:11, which says, "For I know the thoughts that I think toward you, saith the Lord, thoughts of peace, and not of evil, to give you an expected end." It is a blessing to see such a truth unfold.

Chapter 7

A Wonderful Change Has Come Over Me

There is something special about having a personal relationship with Jesus Christ. I will forever be grateful for my wife's love for God because it proved to be a catalyst for me wanting to desire to strengthen my own relationship with Him. I knew that God had great things in store for us. But I also knew that it would be of the utmost importance for me to have my own personal relationship with Him. I would have to be able to know and hear His voice for myself. I would need it for divine direction. This was a journey that I absolutely could not travel without Him. As the business continued to flourish, the way in which God revealed Himself to us played a very key role in its future development.

My desire to know more about the indwelling of the Holy Ghost, which I referenced in the previous chapter, increased over time. We also had many encounters wherein I kept pressing my way until I experienced it for myself. Such encounters began somewhere around 1985 or 1986. Early in our marriage, one of the traditions that Diane and I started was that of hosting a Memorial Day cookout. We would invite my brother, LaGrant, and Diane's brother, Anthony (Tony), and their families. One year, neither LaGrant nor Tony showed up. However, a friend of mine, John Flott, and his wife, Carolyn, and their family did come. We enjoyed a pleasant day of friendship and good food. Before they left, I suggested that we all join hands and pray together. This was a little interesting to experience because it was something I had never done before. Everyone was in agreement, so we gathered ourselves in the living room and prayed.

At that time, Carolyn was already filled with the Holy Ghost. However, as we prayed that evening, something life changing happened. The spirit of the Lord began to rest upon my wife. She didn't speak in tongues, but we knew something was different and we knew we wouldn't have peace until we knew what it was. Thankfully, Carolyn explained what happened. She said the Spirit of the Lord was upon Diane. All she had to do was continue to seek God a little more and she probably would have begun to speak in other tongues.

That following week, Diane wanted to go to a church where what we experienced with John and Carolyn might happen again. Keep in mind that although Diane was a part of the Church of Christ, speaking in tongues was something the Pastor could not provide us with insight on; and we had to seek further guidance in that area. What I learned from that experience is that if you want a steak, you can't go to a hamburger fast food restaurant and get it. What you can get there is a hamburger, which is a form of a steak. However, if you want steak, you have to go where steak is being sold. We weren't going to church that was serving what we so greatly hungered for. If that hunger was going to be satisfied, it would be imperative for us to go to a church that served what we were looking for. That reminds me of 2 Timothy 3:5a, "Having a form of godliness, but denying the power thereof." Many people walk around with a form of holiness without having fully received the gift of the Holy Ghost. Diane was living it – she had, indeed, received it – but she never knew there was more for her spiritually because she wasn't raised to believe that there was more. The ultimate teaching point out of this is the importance of making sure you get all that God has for you, which is the infilling of the Holy Ghost.

I understood what Diane was feeling, so we agreed that she would go to the Lighthouse Church, which was located on Moreland Avenue. (I didn't go because I was at the restaurant working.) Someone had told us about this church and there would be a strong possibility that we could have the kind of spiritual encounter that we were searching for. So Diane went and she stopped by the restaurant afterward. I was standing at the walk-up window when she drove up. As I made my way out to the car, I was hoping to see "that look" on her face, but I didn't. When I got to the car, she confirmed it and told me that it didn't happen again.

Diane and I talked about it more when we got home, but it was almost unexplainable. She went back to the Lighthouse Church the following Friday night. When the service was over, she came to the restaurant again, and I saw that look on her face. When I got to the car, she told me it happened again. She told me the same thing she had experienced before while we were with John and Carolyn happened to her again. This time on my way to the car, I could already see "that look" on her face. We talked about it more when I got home. Although something had clearly happened to her spiritually, she had not begun to speak in tongues at that time.

Later on, Carolyn asked Diane to visit with her at church. She agreed, and this time I went with her. Earlier in the week, Carolyn had already given her the address of where the church was located. We continued with our regular routine during the rest of the week. Sunday came, and we were on our way to church. I thought we were on our way back to the Church of Christ that we had been attending. But as we sat at a red light, I asked my wife, "Where do you want to go to church today?" Her response was that she wanted to take Carolyn up on her offer and visit the church that she and John attended. The name of the church was The Body of Christ Temple on Jones Avenue, and Rev. Lena Davis was the Pastor.

After the service started, the presence of the Lord manifested itself in a mighty, mighty way. It was so strong that the Spirit sat on Diane like I'd never seen it do before: not only was her physical countenance different, but wow...now she was actually speaking in tongues! What a sight to see! I saw Acts 2:4 come alive in Diane. It was just like the Bible says. Although I had read about what it would be like, it was still confusing and somewhat frightening to me because I'd never seen that before. I knew the change that it brought forth was real because I had been living with Diane for approximately five years. Days went by and she was still speaking in tongues. I also noticed that she wanted to pray more. If it wasn't every day, it was just about every day. I knew something had happened, and we continued to go to that church.

My wife continued to speak in tongues, and I continued to see the change in her life. I guess because I had not experienced such a change myself, I began waiting for whatever she was experiencing to be over, but it never was. I later found out that the Pastor was the mother of another one of my close friends. This guy wasn't saved; he didn't seem to be interested in Christ or salvation. But when Pastor Davis found out I knew her son, it seems like that drew her closer to me. She would talk to me about the Word, and she prayed for me.

When I really sat down to think about it, I realized that I wanted what my wife had. In my own way and in my own strength, I tried to get it. After seeing the Spirit of God rest so well on my wife and then not seeing anything happen for me, I was reminded of the idea that the Spirit of God cannot dwell in an unclean place/temple (as described in 1 Corinthians 3:16-17). In other words, I felt within myself that if I truly wanted God to bless me, there would be some wrong things in my life that I would need to make right. I would have to change my way of living by way of my thoughts, words, and deeds. With these thoughts in mind, I tried to get rid of some of my addictions. I still had a few hang ups, but I did stop doing the things I could control.

For example, with me being in the restaurant business, there was always a need for food and food supplies. One of the food items I would often need was chicken strips. Well, there was a local and popular chicken strip manufacturer that would, from time to time, have mis-runs. As such, this opened up the door for me to go by and buy them. Although he wasn't supposed to, the worker would throw extras on my truck and, in appreciation, I would give him a few dollars. One particular day, he had three times more than what he would normally give me. At any other time, I would have gladly taken them, but this time I was convicted. I told him I couldn't take them. That surprised even me because I had a great need for some money that day because I had to pay my Georgia Power bill.

Another incident occurred when I went to Market Grocery. The cashier made a mistake that day and gave me $500-600 more than I was supposed to get back. I couldn't take it either. I didn't know what God was trying to tell me, but I had enough fear of Him not to play games with Him. I would not try my luck with God. That just wasn't going to happen. What I did do was go back to church that night, which was a Tuesday night. I went and I did what the saints of old call "tarry for the Holy Ghost." I prayed, I cried, and I moaned, but I still didn't get it. Weeks passed and still, nothing happened. This began to become really frustrating to me. It was so frustrating that I stopped sitting with my wife during the worship services. Instead, I found myself easing to the back of the church because of my discouragement.

One day as I was sitting in the back of the church, the spirit of the Lord was very high. I raised my hands. I was in my natural mind and in the spirit at the same time, so I knew what was happening to me was not me. I knew what I was experiencing was nothing that was in and of myself. I continued to call on the name of the Lord with my whole heart and soul, and then it happened! I felt like something hit me in the very pit of my stomach. In a way that I cannot explain, unpronounceable words began to come from the innermost part of my being. While I felt like I was still in my natural mind, the unexplainable words that were coming out of my mouth could not be controlled. Then it dawned on me: Acts 2:4 was finally happening to me! I was speaking in tongues as the spirit of God was giving me utterance! What a feeling that was!

It was as if an external force had just taken over my entire being. What was happening was not me. I started feeling something take control of my mouth. As I began to speak, I began to speak in other tongues as the Bible says. As the spirit of God spoke to me, I began to speak. I knew God had taken residence down on the inside of me. Just as the scripture says in 1 Corinthians 14:23, when the church is on one accord and speaking in tongues, others who have not received the gift will think you are crazy. Truly, it is an experience that not everyone accepts. It's very easy to have a form of godliness but also deny the power of the Holy Ghost (2 Timothy 3:5). That's what I had: the power! Acts 1:8 tells us that after you receive the Holy Ghost, you can walk with power. That's exactly how I felt!

Many people don't understand the fact that a person can give their life to the Lord, and when it is time to depart this earthly realm, they can go to heaven. When the Lord Himself left this earth, He sent us a comforter that would take His place here inside of us. It's like a parent leaving a child a will. You have to go get what was left for you. It's like Diane going to the church she was born and raised in. I was a sinner man and knew nothing about the Bible. Yet, I knew what the pastor said was not what God said to me. The pastor was saying something different and I was getting confused. However, Diane couldn't answer the question for me. When we went back to Bible study, I asked the teacher and he said, "That's not what I read." That's where all the curiosity started. It was long awaited and long overdue but so greatly welcomed and appreciated.

Since that day, my life has never been the same. Pastor Davis realized what was happening, and she immediately came to me and she started rejoicing. My wife started rejoicing. The church started rejoicing. That day was like no other day. Nobody can tell me that speaking in tongues is not for today because it happened to me.

Yes, indeed, I knew I had been changed. My wife and Pastor Davis knew it, too. But there will always be those who will doubt. The Bible says some worldly people think you're crazy when you know what you know about the Holy Ghost. I'll never forget how my friend, Alley Pat, said, "It ain't gonna last long. You'll be back in a little bit." I'm pretty sure he was talking about my old ways, which included me smoking marijuana every day. Oh, how I thank God for deliverance from that! I had it bad. I had it so bad that I would pre-roll my joints, make my own packs, and smoke up to a pack a day. I remember leaving home one day without them; somehow I had forgotten them. Maybe it was because the taste for them wasn't there. Whatever it was, it caused me not to come to the realization that I didn't have them until midday. I reached for them only to discover that I didn't have them. The most astonishing thing I discovered was that I didn't have a taste for it. I went on with my regular routine of picking up groceries and supplies for the restaurant. I then went on to work that day and worked like normal. The only thing different was that I just didn't have my joints.

When I got home that evening, I saw that my joints were where I left them; they were still rolled up in the tray waiting on me. They were there for me, but I still didn't have the taste for them. The Lord had taken the taste out of my mouth! I think it was my oldest daughter who asked me one day when I was going to stop smoking. What she did not realize was that God had already taken the taste away from me. I guess neither she nor I realized God was working on me. I kind of chuckled at the thought of me keeping the remaining joints that I had for a while. I did so because I felt like the taste for them would eventually come back. Praise God; it never did! I guess I was doubting myself like Alley Pat was. I flushed the remaining joints down the toilet and never looked back. By all means, a wonderful change had come over me.

Chapter 8

The Costly Anointing

One day, I sat down and really began to think about the many amazing things God has done for me, my family, and This Is It! As I was thinking, my favorite set of words surfaced once again, "What a mighty God we serve!" God has shown Himself strong on our behalf time and time again. I can never take His goodness, grace, mercy, and favor for granted.

However, those who have not been on the front lines with me to get a firsthand look at the various experiences I have had to face along the way may not understand. Perhaps, some may be inclined to believe I was born with a silver spoon in my mouth, so to speak. There may be others who see the blessings of the Lord that have fallen upon us, yet they may not fully understand what it took to get to this point.

The way I see it is that God has given me a gift. He has also anointed me, which enhances the gift. He has favored me to be a part of it all. The anointing is nothing less than a special touch from God. He graces those who are anointed. God will make difficult or challenging things seem simple or effortless for those who experience this combination of anointing, gifting, and favor. However, there is a price to be paid for the anointing. In scripture, the most recognizable symbol of the anointing is oil. If you will notice when Christians conduct an anointing service, the oil that is used is olive oil. Have you ever wondered why? Have you ever even thought about the process of producing oil?

I can tell you that it's not as easy as one may think. First and foremost, the very task of getting an olive from an olive tree is a process all by itself. It's not as simple as picking an apple or an orange from a tree. Olives are very difficult to be picked. Then, once they are picked, it is just as difficult – if not more – to get the oil because olives have to be stepped on, squeezed, and rolled on just to get to the oil. So the next time you see a person that is truly anointed – whether it be in business, the way they sing, teach, preach, dance, speak, cook, do hair, make floral arrangements, or whatever it is that they do so well – please know that they have paid a high price.

The process of getting the oil as was just explained may be compared to the things that anointed people have to go through in order to receive the anointing. For example, many people may say, "Oh, I wish I could sing like Marvin Sapp." Yet, they have no idea of the amount of time he has had to spend in the studio or the ramifications of handling the details of his paperwork as a businessman. They may say, "Oh, I wish I could preach like my Pastor." Yet, if they knew the amount of time their Pastor had to spend studying, not to mention address their other pastoral duties, they may not be so quick to speak.

In the same manner, I have had people to say to me, "Oh, if I had it like you, Mr. Anthony, I would be alright." I'm not so sure about that. Sometimes I tell people, "You couldn't even open my mail. Just opening it would blow you away." Not only that, I remember the times when I had to live with the telephone ringing all night long because security companies were calling to alert me of various emergencies. I finally got to a place (this year) where I could tell the security company not to call me between midnight and 7 a.m.

It doesn't matter what the emergency may be, I am officially out of pocket between those hours. Prior to making that decision, I would have to get up in the middle of the night – sometimes at 2 or 3 in the morning – every time the alarm would go off. I was answering the security company's calls for over 30 years. Keep in mind that this was before cell phones were as popular as they are now, so the calls would come to my home. I asked God to give me another way of handling this.

He did. That is when He instructed me to create set hours wherein the security company would not be permitted to call me.

These are only a few of the sacrifices that I have had to make. There are so many others that come with the territory of trying to build a business. Another is that it's very difficult to make time for yourself. You have to make time for God first, then your family, then your business. It is not uncommon for you to come in fourth or fifth on the chain. At the same time, those on the outside still think your life has been a crystal stair. I'm sure what their minds are alluding to is the glory of what they see from the outside as they look in. But the story behind the glory is a completely different matter. It is a story of great details filled with challenges that the average person just may not be able to handle. I guarantee you that if you read the life story of any great person, if they are truthful, it will not be void of pain, trouble, and adversity.

I am no exception. Being in the restaurant business is no simple task. It requires hard work and long work hours, lots of planning, being available to address frequent emergencies, having accountability, knowing how to use money and credit, and so much more. It is most definitely not something for the faint at heart. You've got to be willing to stick to it and press your way until you can see your way. In addition, you cannot get discouraged when things seem like they will never take off. People will laugh at you, talk about you, and maybe even call you a foolish dream chaser. If I had listened to the negativity, I would not be sharing my story with you today.

I remember facing many days of humiliation as I pursued my dream. One occurred when I was operating Butch's Slide Inn and BBQ. I had left my job at the prescription eyewear company, so the safety net of having a regular paycheck was gone. I'll never forget how hard I was working just to make ends meet. To say that it was hard is making an understatement. I put everything I had into the business: all my time, money, and effort, and it still was a heavy task to take care of the business and my home. Again, making sacrifices is a major part of being in business. It's a sacrifice for food to be in your refrigerator if you need money in the business. It's a sacrifice to bypass buying yourself a suit or shoes if you know you have to pay a bill. There were many days I made those kinds of sacrifices.

Nevertheless, even with all the sacrifices that were being made, there came a time when I was unable to keep things afloat. Cash got so tight that one day I returned home from a long, hard day's work only to discover that all of my belongings had been sat out on the street. I couldn't believe it. I had been evicted because I was late paying my rent! What a great embarrassment that was. I had to pick up the pieces from there and still try to make things work. The image of people picking through my belongings and taking what they could of mine from the street was heartbreaking.

I didn't know God at that time, but He saw fit to bring me through that very turbulent time. It was a major adjustment for me to have to live with somebody for a while. I had no choice but to swallow my pride so that I could try to keep the dream alive. I did persevere, and when God allowed me to stabilize the business again, He also made it clear that the time had come for me to sell the business. After selling the business, I continued to make the BBQ sauce for the new owner; I wouldn't give him the recipe.

Many things transpired during that time, including the passing of my father in 1981. When I met Diane the same year, she brought a different level of joy to my life. It is so very important to have that special someone who will be with you through the good times and the bad; one who will not only say that they understand but show it as well. Diane was in agreement with the direction I chose for our life. She understood the time that it would take and the work that had to be put in to make our dream a reality, and she also made many sacrifices for the sake of the business. I mentioned in a previous chapter how I was unable to buy new dresses for her to wear to church. I'm grateful that she was able to sew her own dresses and that she did not mind making the sacrifice of being without new, store bought dresses.

You can sometimes work so hard that you will find yourself

wondering if God is really there, especially if your faith is not very strong. Despite those thoughts, you just have to keep going. You have to keep trusting and you have to keep believing because giving up is not an option. Until I met Christ for myself and really developed a strong, personal relationship with Him, the best thing I was able to hold on to was my daddy's words that will forever be in my spirit. He told me to go and make the family proud.

Diane and I married in 1983, the same year that we started This Is It! As we began to grow, we saw days of expansion that included bringing on key team players such as John Flott and selling two stores. I was able to get one of the stores back, but I still had to start over again in a new location in the Ben Hill community. We later expanded to the Washington Road location (in the old Waffle House.)

As I reflect on the growth of the business, I am reminded of the long hours and the hard labor. You work long hours every day trying to build something. I know that this business was God's plan for my life because eventually when I met Christ and turned my life over to Him, He started to correct things, work it all out, give me direction, and grant me favor along the way.

Also, my level of spiritual maturity began to increase as time went on. As such, I was further reminded of the story of Job. Many people don't realize that business as a whole can bring trouble. If you are not able to withstand trouble with the hours that the restaurant business requires – or entrepreneurship in general, for that matter – you can't make it. This is especially true with trying to build your own brand.

Job 14:1 says that man that's born of a woman is only on earth for a few days, and those few days are filled with trouble. I can relate to that because I started with nothing. Yet, God turned it into something. He's the only somebody that can do that. It reminds me of God's Word that says, "In the beginning was God." We can conclude from this that there was nothing before Him. There was nothing in the earth. This Is It! was nothing and God turned it into something for His glory. He did it for people to regain hope for whatever they may find themselves going through. Hope is one of the most powerful things we possess as people, but our hope has to be in Jesus Christ in order for it to manifest.

I understand how it feels for things to get rough. I still maintain that you have to rely on and trust in Jesus. The decisions you make will end up being a part of your story. If you make bad decisions, your life will reflect the decisions you've made. Equally, if you make good decisions, your checking account will reflect the decisions you've made as well. Whenever we make decisions, whether they are good or bad, we must also be willing to accept the consequences. For example, I made the decision to quit school in the 10th grade. The only thing I felt like I could do was get what I called "a piece of a job," wherein I made my living by making deliveries for an optical company. I didn't have any other training, so I gladly took the job. I then made another decision to leave the optical business for the restaurant business. I had no choice but to make it work.

Even though I didn't know God at the time, there was still something on the inside that made me keep pushing. I guess it can be attributed to me being an Anthony. I shared earlier that the Anthony men are compulsive. It took me years after conquering my teen gambling problem to learn how to use my compulsion. I had to learn to steer my compulsion in the right direction. The right direction for me was for me to work and try to make the best life for my family as I could. Compulsion is my motivating force. It's what keeps me going. The Bible says that faith without works is dead. You can't say you believe God and expect something to fall from the sky. You have to get out there and make it work. In the process, you should ask God to lead and guide you. The Bible also says that the steps of a good man are ordered by God. Let Him order your steps. I have found that the closer you get to God, the clearer your vision becomes.

As my vision became clearer, God also enhanced my abilities to do well in business, particularly as it relates to how to use money. I clearly understand that money is a tool to get you from point A to point B. You've got to know when to use it and when not to use it. The same thing applies when it comes to using credit. It's a tool. From my perspective, every credit card must be paid off in full each month. If it is not realistic to do so, then my next suggestion is to have a planned date for paying it off. You don't want to pay interest on credit cards.

Unfortunately, credit is a part of life, but this is why your name has to be right. If your name is right, or if your credit is good, it creates the opportunity for you to get the best interest rate when you have to use credit. You need credit in order to build a business because there will be times when you won't be able to pay for everything on the spot. In those times, you should be able to pick up the phone and place a call to a banker or other financier if you need anything. There is absolutely no way you can run a business and every time a vendor pulls up you have to take the money out the register. That's why the Bible says a good name is more valuable than silver and gold. Your name has to be good enough to be, first, written in the lamb's book of life. Then, your name has to be good enough to do business with men you see every day. If your name is no earthly good, how can you represent Christ?

You must realize that you are only going to have one name. You will be born with it, and it will follow you all the way to your grave. What are people going to say when your name comes up in the boardroom or when they look at your credit history? What will people think of your integrity, your character, or your morals? So, indeed, a good name is very important in this life and in your daily walk.

The process of achieving destiny is not always easy, and I have been asked if I ever wanted to give up. I never wanted to give up on my business. I think the closest I've ever come to giving up on anything was the time when I was seeking the Holy Ghost. I was frustrated because I could never get it the way the Bible said I could. I was so frustrated that I got tired of sitting with my wife at church. My frustration caused me to start easing my way to the back of the church. What kept me going was seeing my wife get filled with the Holy Ghost. I knew her before this change came over her, so I knew it wasn't fake. It was her witness that made me want to do whatever it took for God to live on the inside of me. One day he did in 1987.

Not only did God bless my business and grant my heart's desire by filling me with the Holy Ghost, but He also blessed me in spite of my shortcomings. This book's very title expresses the fact that I saw myself as "the underdog." Who would have ever thought that God would have blessed me as greatly as He has, especially considering my educational status? I'm not ashamed to say that even in this fast-paced technological society in which we live, I just tried my hand at texting in 2015. I still don't use computers....but God. I'm living proof that everything that you need is in God. Many people don't know how I can run a company of this size without knowing how to use a computer. People have actually said that to me. When I tell people God has always put around me the right team and all I need to get the job done, I get the special stares.

I've come to realize that most people probably don't do business the way I do. But regardless of what I have or don't have, regardless of my inadequacies, I know that according to Jeremiah 29:11-13, God does have a plan for my life. He has one for you as well. His plan makes it clear that He wants us to have a hope and a future and an expected end. There's one thing that I particularly am encouraged by when I think about the gifts and calling (which are also blessings) of God. Romans 11:29 say that they are without repentance. In other words, you don't have to explain anything about how and why you have been blessed to your haters. That's good news!

As a mature Christian, I am now able to look back on situations later and realize the difficult things I have had to endure were part of the things God was using to make me better. It was part of the price I had to pay for the costly anointing. I love the way the Amplified Bible explains Proverbs 5:1. It basically says that someone has paid a cost for us. All we have to do is pay attention. The cost of the anointing has commanded my full attention. And because I'm still standing and still prospering God's way and by God's grace, I know that there is nothing too hard for Him. He has blessed. I am grateful. And the best is yet to come.

Chapter 9

The Unforgettables

It has been said that in order to be a success, you must see a success. I believe that to be true. There are many lessons to be learned by watching others who have trodden the paths that you desire to tread. You can make observations on what works well and what may not work so well. Every situation may not be the same, but I have found the foundational principles to be universal. They can be used and applied in a way that the effects are the same. Perhaps this is one of the understandings of the scripture that says there is nothing new under the sun.

In my lifetime, I have had the privilege of knowing some people for a long time, if not all my life. Then there are others that God allowed me to meet along the way. I call these special people "The Unforgettables." Of course, the person who has had the greatest impact on me in terms of molding me as a businessman is my father. I spent many days and nights in the restaurant with him learning the ins and outs of the restaurant business. He taught me many invaluable lessons on everything from how to handle money to how to deal with people to birthing vision.

As it relates to money, my father had a lock box. Inside the lock box was also a cigar box, which is where he kept a lot of his money. I remember there being silver dollars, half dollars, and special coins that he was saving. It's funny how history has a way of repeating itself. After having gotten older, I found myself saving silver dollars, half dollars, and old coins just as my father had done. His influence was ever meaningful. I will forever remember and appreciate the stamp of approval he gave when he told me to *"go and make the family proud"* upon me telling him of my desire to leave Tampa and begin a different journey.

In addition to my father, there were other businessmen whom I had the opportunity to observe from a distance as I was growing up. You may recall from chapter 2 that one of the neighborhoods we grew up in was full of role models we could emulate. This experience presented a great opportunity for young kids to see people who looked like them work hard and make a decent living for their families. Two people that come to mind are Mr. Bexley and Mr. Mose White. Both of these men were well-established businessmen. Looking at them gave me hope. As a young boy growing into manhood, it was a good thing for me to see them and know that with hard work and perseverance, I could be successful just like them.

When I moved to Atlanta, I was able to see others who were doing just as well as Mr. Bexley and Mr. White. One such person was my friend, Alley Pat, whom I also talked about earlier (in chapter 6.) Through my friendship with Alley Pat, I not only got a chance to see what it looked and felt like to run a successful enterprise, but I also began to realize the importance of developing and cultivating relationships. He was a businessman, but our relationship as friends was just as important as it was to each other as businessmen. He was a mentor as well as someone I could look up to, share concerns with, and just be transparent with so that I could get through whatever I may have had to face from time to time.

It is always good to learn from those whom you know, but there are also lessons that can be learned from afar. For example, in the 1980s, right after I met Diane, we found ourselves frequenting a very popular restaurant. It ended up being one of our favorite spots for eating fish. Well, one Saturday night when I was in there, the Lord showed me that

He would one day bless us beyond anything that I had ever seen. He showed me that He would use me to create something that would be major, right there in our community.

This revelation, within itself, was amazing to me because I really did not know the Lord at that particular time. Granted, I had begun attending church regularly as a result of me dating Diane, but I could not say that I was in a relationship with God then. For God to be giving me insight and intuition on what was to come was truly amazing. He allowed me to see the time that we spent in this establishment as somewhat of a business model. Remember, one person's success can inspire others to pursue their own success. Although I didn't know the owner, I was still able to come in our community and learn from someone who was already doing what I knew I would one day be doing as well.

Another business model I learned from was that of Mr. V., owner of Mr. V's Figure 8 Night Club. Like the owner of the fish place, Mr. V. was also another person that I looked up to, even though I didn't meet him until many years later. When I started out in business, I used to look at his business model and marvel at how successful he was. He really thrived tremendously back in the day. People who have been in Atlanta for a while or have history with the city know that Mr. V's club on Campbellton Road was the place where all the athletes and entertainers came. Now that I think about it, Mr. V's could very well have been one of the catalysts that helped Atlanta become dubbed "HotLanta" and "Hollywood of the South." If you were a celebrity, a celebrity in the making, a "wannabe" celebrity, or if you just wanted to be on the celebrity scene, Mr. V's was the place to be.

After years of watching Mr. V. from afar, I finally met him; and I do some business with him today. The club is not operational anymore, but he owns a place called Mr. V's Restaurant Equipment. I talk to him, and I'm so honored and humbled that he was one of the people that God led me to minister. In the process, he gave his life to Christ. What happened was that when I called him one day, I discovered he was in the hospital. As I left a message for him, I found myself praying for him. When we finally talked, he told me no one had ever done that before. At that very moment, we formed a different kind of relationship; it seemed like we had a deeper connection. God used me to help lead him to Christ!

Others amongst "The Unforgettables" was a beautiful couple that was probably well into their 80s: Mr. and Mrs. Richardson. Many years ago, Mr. Richardson was the president of Citizens Trust Bank. He and his wife used to eat with us in the first restaurant. One day, I asked them to appear in a commercial for me. I figured it would be a good fit because they were such loyal patrons of the restaurant. It was also a great honor to have a prominent couple – who were also leaders in the community – to endorse us by appearing in a TV commercial on behalf of our business. This was exciting to me because it presented an opportunity to show successful Black people in a TV commercial supporting a Black-owned business.

What was probably just as exciting was the approach we took with the commercial. Similar to the popular 1980s Wendy's "Where's the Beef" commercial, our commercial featured a couple in their 80s. Just as the elderly lady in the Wendy's commercial was inquiring about beef, the Richardsons were talking about fish. And so it was: I used these 80-something year old customers to say, "Here's the fish!" They were so proud to be a part of it, and I was proud to have them be a part of it as well.

Mr. Richardson was very helpful in many ways, but Mrs. Richardson was just as special. She was one of those ladies who was very prominent in the community; she was part of a number of auxiliaries and an outstanding citizen. When she would go to various places to speak, we would go and prepare the food for her. They would never charge us for anything they did for us. As they got older and older, we would always make sure they had fish to eat. We especially enjoyed delivering the fish (that they loved so well) to them, and it was our honor to do so whenever they called. Mr. Richardson passed away at age 90 or so, and we would still take fish and cole slaw to Mrs. Richardson after that time. I will never forget the great inspiration they were to us.

Another "Unforgettable" was Ed Neely. God used him to partner with me to buy our first shopping center. I like to call it our first "piece of dirt." Ed used to be the person that I would buy food for the restaurant through, so I already knew him. God used him in the late 1990s to come to me and tell me that he knew I would one day buy the whole shopping center on Memorial Drive, which is the location of where the restaurant was and still is located today. He said he knew that Memorial Drive was a good location for the shopping center and the restaurant. If the opportunity presented itself for me to own the shopping center – which he seemingly thought I one day would – and because he believed so strongly in what we were doing, he wanted to be a part of it.

Later on, my relationship with the owner of the shopping center grew. His name was Edwin Larkin, and he trusted me enough to ask me to help him keep an eye on the shopping center. I would let him know what was needed and keep him abreast of any other matters that may have required his attention. As time went on, he would invite me to his home, and we began to talk on a regular basis. During our many conversations, he would tell me about things that happened in his life. I learned that his father left him a real estate empire to run for the family after his passing. The number of properties and his growth as a businessman caused him to be involved with all kinds of business deals. Accordingly, he would talk to me about some of the deals he was doing and different ideas that were on his mind.

As time went on, Edwin told me, "Shelley, if I had my way, I would just give you this shopping center so you can see life from a different perspective." But, it wasn't up to him; he could not have his way because he had to report to his sisters, and rightfully so. I remember him telling me about one of his sisters being saved and Holy Ghost-filled. She had to remind him that their father had entrusted him to make sure business operations remained intact so that they would continue to have their finances in order and live without worry. Nevertheless, he still trusted me enough to talk to me. I think he just needed to have a different perspective on things from time to time. He still remembered his sister's admonitions, but God gave me favor with him, which really and truly let me know that God can touch one person's heart on your behalf and change your whole life forever.

Ed (Larkin) and I continued to talk, and he came to me one day to discuss a new business idea. The shopping center (on Memorial Drive) was always full of tenants other than one spot on the end. There had been a vegetable stand previously, but it went out of business. We talked about it, and I suggested we do a pizza restaurant. Ed agreed and invested all the money for me to open Shelley's Pizza. We got it up and running, but unfortunately, I couldn't make it work. It was out of my lane, and I finally accepted the fact that I just didn't know the pizza business.

About a year later, we decided to close the pizza restaurant. Ed sold it, and the new owners opened a Chinese restaurant. For someone to go to the extreme of investing six figures (approximately $200k) in you to open a business simply because they like you was extraordinary. The fact that the business didn't survive was disappointing, but it taught me the valuable lesson of learning to "stay in your lane" in business. It is of great importance to stick to what you know how to do. If you don't know how to do something that you want to do, at least learn as much as you can about it before taking the plunge. You must keep in mind that your family's livelihood and other families are at stake.

A few years later, somewhere between 1998 and 1999, I began to see a need to make some changes for my family. I had a couple of pieces of rental property. They had served their purpose well, but I began to desire to put my family in another house. As I began to ponder how I could do this, I decided to sell the rental property so I could build a house and an office. Even with me selling the property, I would still have to pull together other financial resources in order, to make sure we had things in order as they would need to be. Therefore, in addition to cashing in on the rental properties, I also cashed in on the funds that I had in the stock market.

In the meantime, Ed Larkin came to me and said, "I want you to have this shopping center. It's not for sale, but I want you to have it." I knew that if I was going to purchase the shopping center, I would need an estimated amount of $200,000+. I told him I didn't have that kind of money; I had just invested a good deal of money in trying to build my family a house. My friend, Ed Neely (whom I mentioned earlier in this chapter and who also happened to be in real estate), came to me and again said he felt like I was going to own the shopping center one day and that he wanted to be a part of it when that time came.

I began to think about what Ed Neely said as well as what Ed Larkin had said. God gave me a plan concerning these things, so "I wrote it down" and continued to think. During this time, I had completed the construction of the house, but we didn't move in it right away. I was in the process of planning for a big catering event at boxing champion Evander Holyfield's home. He chose us to provide the food for his annual 4th of July cookout. This was a very popular event that was attended by what seemed to be everybody in Atlanta. What an honor it was to know that he chose us! It was one of the biggest jobs I had ever done. I think we fed approximately 2,000 people that day on his estate.

After we got through this event is when we moved into the new house. I felt like the time had come for me to pick back up the conversation I had begun with Ed Larkin. I knew I needed to get someone to go into this deal with me because I didn't have that kind of money. Who could I consider to partner with me? I thought about reaching out to one of my neighbors. Because I knew he made a decent living for himself, I figured the likelihood of him having the necessary financial resources would be high. But I thought that asking him would be a little shaky because we were not equally yoked. He was a good guy, but being good without Christ is a paved road to hell.

If I was going to consider this deal, I would need to think quickly. That is when I remembered Ed Neely. He was in my life, and I knew he was saved. And even though my neighbor probably would have been financially able to support the effort far greater than Ed Neely would, wisdom taught me it would be in my best interest to work the deal with someone with whom I was equally yoked, as the Bible says. Ed Neely was saved, so I knew I had to go in that direction.

This all took place around Thanksgiving in 2000. The Sunday before Thanksgiving is when Ed Neely came to my door. In response to our previous conversations, he was ready to move on the deal. He brought me cashier's checks for $200,000 and said, "Butch, this is all the money I've worked for all my life. I just want to be a part of this deal."

When I called Ed Larkin and told him, he said, "Shelley, I'm going to try and get it worked out." It only took him a few days to call me back and tell me he had it worked out. As we went forth with the deal, I wanted at least 60% of it. Ed Neely wanted a little more. By the time we worked it all out, Ed Neely had 49%, and I had 51%. The bottom line was that I wanted to have the last word when decisions needed to be made.

When Ed Neely and I worked everything out, I proceeded to talk to Ed Larkin, and he came up with a closing date. We met him at a SunTrust Bank in Duluth. I told Ed Larkin how much money I had and that I was short of the amount he had originally told me was needed. He had already told the lady who was doing the paperwork how he wanted to build the structure of the financing. When she came with the paperwork, it was clear that we needed more money than what we had. He told the banker that he didn't want me to pay any more than what I had. This caused her to think something fishy was going on. She said, "Mr. Larkin, we've been doing business together for a long time, and we've never done anything like this. I've been closing commercial real estate for 28 years and I've never seen a deal like this." This was a professional woman, and I did not believe she would do anything to compromise her career or her integrity. Neither is this something that any of us wanted or expected. She proceeded to do her job, and I walked out of there owning 51% of that shopping center without putting up any money of my own. God just worked it out!

Without a doubt, Ed Neely is the one God used to bring the first manifestation of Deuteronomy 1:8 in my life to pass. *(Deuteronomy 1:8 says, "Behold, I have set the land before you: go in and possess the land which the Lord sware unto your fathers, Abraham, Isaac, and Jacob, to give unto them and to their seed after them.")* I will never forget that; I will forever be grateful. A few years later when Ed Neely wanted out of the deal, God gave me a plan that allowed us to negotiate what to do and how to do it. Again, "I wrote it down." I was able to refinance the property and release him from the deal, as he desired. *Today, I own that property 100%, and I was able to do it without an earthly partner. I will always maintain that my partner in all that I do, my ultimate and eternal partner, is Jesus Christ.*

This is just one of the many reasons why relationships are so important. But an even more important relationship is the one we have with Jesus. In fact, it is the most important of all. I know for a fact that He will direct you. *That's why Psalm 37:5 – which speaks of committing one's ways to the Lord, trusting Him, and knowing that He will bring things to pass – is important.* God will put people in your path for a season to do business with. God gave me a burden for Ed Larkin's soul. We used to sit in the parking lot and pray for him and the things he had dealt with. Generally speaking, he was raised a Catholic. He was a multimillionaire, and he had everything that the world could possibly offer. Yet, out of everything he had, he didn't have Christ in the fullness. As I dealt with him, I do believe the fact that his sister was saved helped draw him closer to Christ. Our spirits connected, and we both knew the importance of having a relationship with Jesus. I think in my own way, I was hoping that he would come to know and embrace Jesus Christ in a more intimate way.

Pastor Emeritus Ronald Moore is another "Unforgettable." He was a very inspirational person in my life. He was one that God showed me was one of His miracles. However, I didn't know he was a miracle until God revealed it to me after his passing. I will reference him in greater detail in the "Defining Moments" section of the book, but for now, I have to tell you again how different and special he was. To know that he faced a 23-year heroin addiction, yet was able to get delivered without rehab, get his family back, and go on to become pastor of Welcome All Community Church was beyond admirable; it was truly a great example of the power of God. It was nothing short of miraculous!

I am further reminded of DeCarlos Spenser, another employee who recently passed away. DeCarlos worked for me for more than 20 years. He was in his early 40s when he transitioned, but the life he lived was a wonderful representation of God's grace and mercy. God showed me that if DeCarlos had not come through This Is It!, he might not have been saved; he might not have gotten the Word. DeCarlos, I believe, was saved because of the many times God allowed me to witness to him. That's what God uses this business for; for people to come through and learn of Him. That's why I say I do kingdom building work first, and then I sell food. And, I am ever-inspired by Matthew 6:33, which says, "Seek ye first the kingdom of God and his righteousness, and all these things shall be added unto you."

Two other "Unforgettables" are Pastor John Flott and Pastor John Nash. (I referenced Pastor Flott in chapters 7 and 8, and I will share more about Pastor Nash in chapter 11.) It's good to have people in your life who know Christ; who are true believers of Christ who are not just around you for what they think they can get. Being around people who have a genuine love for God and people is a blessing, indeed.

In addition to blessing me to have relationships with some very wonderful people, God has also allowed me to see several miracles in other areas of my life. I will talk about the personal miracles of how God saved me from the car accident and how he healed my body in chapter 10. Earlier in this chapter, I shared with you the great blessing that took place at the Memorial Drive property. God also did some powerful things with our locations at Camp Creek MarketPlace, Panola, Road and Mount Zion. *For example, with Camp Creek, God allowed me to tie up a million-dollar piece of property with just $5,000.* In so doing, He walked me through that process in a way that only He could. I still stand in total awe of how great my God is!

The visions God gives me for building these projects are simply phenomenal. Morever, to know that He's able to do what He does through me with the educational background that I have is even more phenomenal. Again, I have to tell you that it's all about relationships, especially the relationship we have with God. I know for a fact that God puts me in the presence of people who can make a difference. As I interact with them, He gives me wisdom and favor. That's the biggest thing: **FAVOR.** I know that the favor of God rests upon my life and my business ventures. It always shows up in helping me do what I do. God showed me where He owns favor; He can do with it what He desires. I'm thankful that He allows it to fall into my life.

My personal relationship with Jesus Christ reminds me that one of the best ways to stay close to God is by praying, meditating, and reading His Word and believing every word of it. The Bible is the number one selling book in the world. It was written by God through the inspiration of The Holy Ghost, according to 2 Timothy 3:16, which says, "All scripture is given by inspiration of God, and is profitable for doctrine, for reproof, for correction, for instruction in righteousness:" You just have to believe that. There is a lot in the Bible that you will not understand, just as there is a lot in the Bible that you may not know. However, I have learned that if the Lord says it, you must believe it and ask God to give you revelation knowledge about what that Word means pertaining to your life. Most people don't go to the Bible until they get in trouble. If you start with it, you'll know you have some help and better direction.

As I go forth from day to day and watch my legacy unfold, my prayer is that God will bless my children and grandchildren with double the favor that He gave me. I like to stand on Proverbs 13:22, which says, "A good man leaves an inheritance for his children's children." And please keep in mind that this inheritance is not solely restricted to finances. God wants to give us the inheritance of salvation, integrity, a good name character, faithfulness and so many other good virtues. If you are truly void of these things, it makes it very challenging to appreciate the finances when they come. That's why I always tell my youngest son, who has my name, "You must be careful with how you live and what you do because you carry my name. People will expect you to live a certain way."

I choose to trust and believe that my seed will be blessed with the same type of double portion anointing that God has bestowed upon me. That's the importance of us knowing Jesus Christ because we can reference different things in the Bible that happened in the Bible days and be reassured that the same thing can happen for us today (1 Corinthians 10:11). Therefore, I believe that my children can experience that anointing. I believe that my seed is going to have double. I pray that everybody that is under the umbrella of the This Is It! Family will trust God and have the favor of God on their life. At my recent birthday celebration, my oldest son wrote in his birthday card to me that he just hoped that he could be half the man that I am. I told him, "I believe you will be more. You're on my back, so to speak, like I was on my daddy's back." In order to go and make the family proud, I had to be able to do more. I expect my children to do more and be better. And they'll have to do it for Christ's sake so that people will see what Jesus Christ has done in the Anthony family. It's about God getting the glory for everything that has been done. That's what I want my children and grandchildren to know. The ones who chose not to be a part of this business are living beneath their privilege.

As with any endeavor, there have been some missteps. One of the biggest missteps for me was when God told me not to sign the lease in the West End Mall, and I signed it anyway. (See chapter 6.) That deal proved to me that even though sometimes things may look good, God is the only somebody that knows what the future is going to hold. That deal was most definitely a misstep. It took me six or seven years to regain solid footing after that ordeal.

A retrospective look at moves made in business will also cause you to reflect upon things you wish you had done but then chose not to. For example, I pass by buildings and properties that I should have bought but didn't. Sometimes you just don't take the time to seek God like you should because you are in a hurry or whatever the case might be. Of course, you will have feelings of "what if" for things that you could have taken advantage of that have had positive results for others. When this happens, you can't let it get you down. I have learned to chalk such situations up and view them as being "water under the bridge."

If you're going to live for Christ, you must be willing to go through difficult situations. It's not an easy walk. You will miss some things, but you will also get some things right. The good news is that at the end of the day, God's got our back. We have the miracles He has performed as evidence, and we also have invaluable relationships as well as favor with God and men. This is a wonderful combination, and I appreciate it working well in my life.

And even as I put pen to paper in writing this book, I am asking God for the wisdom, vision, and foresight to reposition This Is It! BBQ and Seafood for the next 20 years of growth. I have to seek Him as I ponder where the locations should be as I shift into new markets, relocate some stores, and launch **This Is It! BBQ America.** I am also counting on God to help me as I make decisions on the right people to be close to me. Sometimes people that are close to you are not really with you wholeheartedly. I have learned that you have to believe God will shine a light on them in His time. I am also counting on God to help me choose the right franchisees to help tell their own story of what God can do. I know He can do it, and I know that He will. The journey continues, and I stand firm in knowing that eyes have not seen and neither have ears heard the things God has prepared for them that love Him and has prepared for This Is It! BBQ and Seafood.

Chapter 10

The Exceptionally Unforgettable

In the previous chapter, I shared with you many of "The Unforgettables" of my life. Each of the people and experiences that I shared will never escape my memory. As memorable and impactful as each of those "Unforgettables" was, it may be hard to believe that there are any others that could possibly surpass them; yet, there are. I have chosen to call them "The Exceptionally Unforgettable." In Proverbs 18:16, the Bible speaks of a person's gift making room for them and putting them before great men. I witnessed this personally on many occasions, but there are three in particular of which I am especially proud. This is why I call them "The Exceptionally Unforgettable." These people and times are: (1) being featured on the Ice T and Coco Show and winning the BBQ contest, (2) being voted Best BBQ in America in Steve Harvey's 2011 Hoodie Awards, and (3) meeting three outstanding Americans on the same night: Oprah Winfrey, Tyler Perry and President Barack Obama.

The first "Exceptionally Unforgettable" I'd like to share occurred in 2015. It was a great joy to receive a phone call wherein we were asked if we were interested in being a part of the Ice T and Coco Show. This would be a talk show hosted by the legendary rap artist, Ice T and his wife, Coco. For those of you who may not know, Ice T is one of the very first rappers to hit the scene when the genre (rap) made its debut in the 1980s. He is also an actor who appeared in the movie, "New Jack

City." His work in the television series "New York Undercover" earned him a NAACP Award for Outstanding Supporting Actor in a Drama Series (1996).

Therefore, to receive a call from the show's producers was no small matter. This would be wonderful. It would actually be a blessing that would give us national exposure. The reason for them approaching us was because they wanted to have a BBQ contest. I am grateful that our reputation paved the way for us. They had heard that we have a great brand of BBQ, so they thought it would be fitting for us to be a part of that particular episode. That was good news all by itself!

It was our honor to accept this new and exciting opportunity. Perhaps the even bigger blessing was the fact that the opportunity presented itself to us without us having to seek it. As part of us being a part of the show, we were flown into New York City and placed in a hotel. We had to send the food partially prepared before we left, and we had to finish it when we got there and settled. That was a new experience for us, but certainly, it was something we were able to handle with God's help.

Meeting Ice T and Coco was a good experience. We got a chance to talk to them and see that they are everyday people just like anyone else. Being on the set of the show was a good thing, too. I have had the opportunity to be featured in the New York Times, on CNN, and the local channels of 5 and 11 here in Atlanta, but there's something extra special about being on the set of a talk show. I got a chance to see all the behind the scenes details that at-home audiences generally don't see.

When the time finally came, my son, Telley, and I represented This Is It! BBQ and Seafood. We were up against others, but we were not afraid of the competition. We stood strong in the boldness and confidence of the Holy Spirit. Whether we won or lost, we still counted it a blessing and even an honor to be considered. Do you know how many BBQ restaurants there are in America? Talk about favor! We believed God truly favored us just by giving us such an opportunity. It would be a wonderful thing for us to win, but we also knew that if we did not, we were already winners just by being there. We trusted God and were willing to accept whatever the outcome may have been. Nevertheless when the taste test was done by Ice and Coco, and the announcement was made that we won, we were ecstatic! At that moment, I can say that I could understand the Williams Brothers (Gospel recording artists) when they sang the song, "Ooooh wee! Another Blessing!"

I say it was another blessing because another honor similar to that which was bestowed upon us on the Ice T and Coco Show took place in 2011. Renowned comedian turned radio host, turned TV talk show and game show host, Steve Harvey started an awards show years ago called "The Hoodie Awards," which is now called "The Neighborhood Awards." The awards basically existed for the purpose of recognizing every day businesses in the Black community. Oftentimes, the owners of such businesses rarely get the recognition that is so greatly deserved. In 2011, we had the honor of being nominated in two categories for The Hoodie Awards: Best Soul Food and Best BBQ.

It cannot go without saying that the Hoodie Awards nomination was another prayer answered. Some time ago, I prayed that God would use an entertainer or athlete to reach back and endorse a small Black-owned business that serves the community in our continual efforts to grow. This was a prayer I prayed for many years. And I wasn't asking for selfish reasons; it didn't have to be This Is It! *I just knew in my heart and soul that there was a whole world of small, Black-owned businesses in many American communities that rarely get the recognition deserved. I just wanted to see someone come forth and show to the world that we exist and that we are making a difference.* God answered this prayer by not only presenting This Is It! with two nominations, but a large number of categories gave several other businesses the opportunity to be nominated as well.

The way the Hoodie Awards works is that Mr. Harvey would announce one of the many different categories every day on the Steve Harvey Morning (radio) Show. Listeners would be instructed on how to go online and vote for the company of their choice in each of the categories. It would be up to the nominees to solicit the support of customers, family, friends, and others to vote on their behalf. This takes place months in advance of the actual awards ceremony. Winners are announced live during the evening of the awards ceremony.

The 2011 Hoodie Awards took place in Las Vegas, Nevada at the Mandalay Bay Events Center. Just as we were flown in and put in a hotel like we were for the Ice T and Coco Show, the same accommodations were made for us at The Hoodies. However, I must say that the hotel accommodations were much grander. It was simply exquisite. The time leading up to the awards ceremony was very exciting. All the nominees got a chance to go to a special event called "The White Ball." We also got a chance to walk the red carpet as we made our entrance into the main event.

When it was time for the winners to be announced, we came in second in the category of Best Soul Food. And that was okay; we were grateful. But when the winner was announced for Best BBQ, we were ecstatic to hear that the winner was This Is It! BBQ and Seafood! Beyond the shadow of a doubt, God had worked another wonder on our behalf. This is an accomplishment that I will never forget.

Ranking among these two "Exceptionally Unforgettables" are the experiences I had of meeting Oprah Winfrey, Tyler Perry and President Barack Obama on the same night. This experience was an epic moment! When the President came to Atlanta in 2012, I had an opportunity to meet him. Only a select few individuals were chosen to meet him; it would take place at Tyler Perry's house. Naturally, I was excited and elated to have been extended an invitation. We also supported the President, so the invitation made it all the more special. After I got there and went through all the high levels of security, I was totally surprised to be greeted at the door by the one and only media mogul, Oprah Winfrey. When she opened the door, it was more than a notion for me to walk into her presence. She said, "Come on and let me show you around." After she showed me around, there may have been 10-15 people who were there already. For God to choose me to be in that number to meet the President was more than I could have ever imagined.

After Oprah continued to converse with the guests, I had a chance to engage in small talk with her. I was reminded of the early days of my entrepreneurial journey. I was given a chance to advertise during the time of day when her show was on the air. I was still a fairly new business at the time, but there was a young man who worked in sales at channel 2, the station on which The Oprah Winfrey Show aired in Atlanta. He taught me how to ask for "unsold inventory," which basically meant commercial time slots that had not been bought. At that time, there was unsold inventory during the time Oprah's show was on; the commercial slots in her beginning in Atlanta were not always sold out. This presented an opportunity for me to purchase commercials that would air during the Oprah Winfrey show at a very affordable cost.

This was a blessing while it lasted. As God continued to bless Oprah and enlarge her territory, there came a time when the advertising rates were not as affordable as what I was able to take advantage of through the purchase of unsold inventory. I wanted so badly to tell Oprah how blessed I was to be able to advertise with her during the early days. She was standing on one side of the room and I was on the other side. Before I knew it, I said, "Hey, Oprah. Come here. I want to tell you something." I had to catch myself. Surprisingly, she came on over and we began to talk. As much as I wanted to have a "regular conversation" with her, I had to keep in mind that this was not an "everyday person" to me. I mean, this was Oprah Winfrey: superstar celebrity Oprah Winfrey. I couldn't just talk to her as if she was my sister or something. I was talking to Oprah Winfrey, and if I wanted to share that story with her, I knew I would have to choose my words carefully and wisely. I also didn't want to make her feel like she had priced me out of the market.

In talking to Oprah, she began to share with me and others. To my surprise, she opened up and shared some of the difficulty she had in dealing with people. She told us that, because of the success that she had achieved, people started hating on her. She also shared how she had to face some difficult days with the network she started. It was encouraging and comforting to have had this conversation with her. Just listening to her talk helped me to realize that she had faced the same kinds of scenarios that I go through; hers were just at another level. Just hearing firsthand that a person as accomplished as Oprah Winfrey also endured the same kind of challenges as I do only confirmed the importance of believing in what you're doing. It was very inspirational and empowering, to say the least.

Many of the tips I will share in principle 14 of chapter 12 fit into the conversation I had with Oprah. You cannot let people distract you. Most people don't want to see you succeed. That's why it's important to ask God to show you who needs to be close to you. By engaging in conversation with her, it let me know that I was on the right track. You can't let people discourage you. I have found, many times over, that if a person can't do what they see you doing in business, envy will cause them not to want to see you succeed. You have to stay focused, and your eyes have to stay focused on Jesus Christ. God knows how to get you through whatever you have to go through.

Another highlight of the night was meeting Tyler Perry. He struck me as a very humble and down to earth person that you could have a conversation with. As the host for the gathering, he was very welcoming...he was an outstanding host. During our conversation, I talked to him about the people at his studio and how they support the restaurant. I appreciate Tyler for making the decision to launch his studio in the Greenbriar area.

I'm not sure if he realizes it or not, but what he has done is put something in the community that allows us to be supportive of one another. This is not merely a move that will only benefit entertainers. People are coming in from all over the country just to be a part of the new Atlanta entertainment mecca. There is something for everyone to do or be a part of. To me, that is outstanding.

It is not uncommon for Tyler's actors and staff members to frequent our Camp Creek location. Sometimes they have lunch there and sometimes they order catering from us. I do appreciate him and his team for being very supportive of us. I have even been in conversations previously with David and Tamela Mann about the possibility of him doing a This Is It! commercial.

As the evening progressed, we had dinner. When it was time for the President to come, everyone had to turn off their cell phones because the use of electronic devices was prohibited. After all the security was cleared, members of the Secret Service came in and then the President made his entrance. Upon his arrival, we all got a chance to shake his hand and talk to him one on one. His photographer took pictures of us and made sure we all got our copies. I still have the picture of me shaking his hand.

In listening to the President talk, it was like he had a chance to have a normal conversation. It wasn't as if it is when "his people" have to prepare him to make a formal speech. He didn't have to watch his words. He spoke like one of the guys. It was a conversation that was different from what you see on TV. That was an experience that I will never forget. The more President Obama talked, the more I began to think about the blessing it was of being in his presence. I thought to myself, "Here I am, just a regular guy that's out here trying to make a living and take care of his family and be a blessing to other families that's around me with the incredible blessing of meeting the President of the United States." It felt surreal.

Not only did we get a chance to meet him then, but we later received an invitation to come to the White House for a Christmas party. We accepted the invitation. The food was outstanding and the décor was captivating. Thinking on these things brings humility because something like that seems so out of reach for a normal, everyday person. But yet God chose me. I remember what God spoke in my spirit. He said He owns favor, and He can do with it what He chooses. He chose me to have dinner in the White House with the first African American President of these United States of America.

Again, God can put you amongst whomever He wants to put

you amongst, with no explanation. I believe He does it so that we can experience life from a different perspective. I counted it an absolute blessing to be able to tour the White House, behold the many artifacts of American history and to get a firsthand look at the many contributions made by our previous Presidents.

Standing in complete awe of our President and his accomplishments, I was compelled to have a card made that shows how God allowed me, under President Barack Obama's administration, to build three shopping centers and employ approximately 100 people. Keep in mind that this happened during the so-called "Great Recession" of our time. This made it clear to me that, in God's house, there is no recession. We had our best years during this so-called "Great Recession."

We have also been able to purchase additional land. (I will talk about the land in greater detail in the next chapter.) It was a tedious process, but God has brought it to pass, nevertheless. The property is located at 415 North Glenn Street in the city of Fayetteville, GA. It's within a quarter of a mile from our corporate office.

Construction on the new site is now complete! It is a new This Is It! stand-alone franchise model. This is a tremendous accomplishment, and it truly serves as further evidence of that fact that when you represent Christ, there is no recession in His house. You may not be able to escape the reality of the struggles that will come along the way, but we must always hold on to hope. I know for sure that the devil is warring very hard in an effort to discourage me from doing all I can to bring to pass that which God has promised me. Something on the inside would always rise up and push me to keep going and remind me of the fact that this initiative would be a blessing to others. This is why the struggle is so real. I found comfort in knowing that, just as the Bible says, Jesus is the same today, yesterday and forevermore. He is ever faithful. What a blessing and joy it is to see Him bring His promises to pass!

When the night was over, I felt overjoyed. What an experience! On the way home, the Lord started speaking to my spirit, and the words He spoke to me came from Ephesians 3:20, "Don't ever forget that I can do exceeding abundantly above all that you could ever ask or imagine according to the power that works on the inside of you," is what He said to me. This let me know that if you don't have anything working on the inside, nothing's going to show up on the outside.

Clearly, it crossed my mind: how could I ever imagine having a social engagement with the President of the United States, Oprah Winfrey and Tyler Perry on the same night at Tyler's estate? How could I ever imagine being on platforms presented by Ice T and Coco and Steve Harvey? It was then that I realized God was showing me what He can do. That's why we have to trust Him, believe Him and walk with Him. This is just a part of my journey with Christ.

Chapter 11

The Faith Factor

The love of God is amazing to me. I will always be grateful for having Him to come into my heart and rest, reign and rule over me. Beyond the shadow of a doubt, the faith factor has been and remains a very key aspect of my life. I acknowledge that without God I am nothing. There is no way I could amount to anything without His help. I like how Psalm 37:23 puts it. It says that the steps of a good man are ordered by God. I believe that in order for one's steps to be ordered, wisdom must be present. According to Proverbs 4:7, wisdom is the principal thing. Further, the Bible encourages us that out of any and everything we can possibly get out of life, getting an understanding from the wisdom gained should be amongst our top priorities.

I have learned that the wisdom of God is something we don't have unless we have a close relationship with Him. THIS IS IMPORTANT because it allows God to speak to us and give us direction on what we need to do. Yes, indeed, wisdom is huge. In my life, I try to rely on the Word of God to give me direction. The way I see it, I operate with the Master Computer, THE ONE who put everything together. You see, God's wisdom is the master mainframe because in the beginning, there was God; there was nothing else. The book of Jeremiah tells us that God knew us first. And because He took the time to make us – we are His handiwork – not only did He know us, but we should also understand and embrace the fact that He has a plan for our life. I wish everyone could rejoice in knowing that before their mother knew their father, God knew them and He had the ultimate plan for their life. That is an unexplainable feeling!

Just as I mentioned in chapter 10, I am always mindful of the fact that God is able to do exceeding abundantly above all that we could ever ask or imagine according to the power that works on the inside of us. If there is nothing on the inside, then God has nothing to work with; that's the only way something can show up on the outside. It is so very important to really and truly know that. Again, the only way to walk in this truth is to have a personal relationship with God. To that end, I maintain that the wisdom of God is beyond anything. You can run on that all day and all night. The wisdom of God has shown me that God is more than enough. In fact, He is all that you need.

Once you are assured of your relationship with God, it is also very important to make certain that your prayer life is intact. Prayer is nothing less than communicating with God: you talk to Him and He talks to you. Take the time to talk to Him, but also take the time to listen to what He has to say to you. It is then, in times of prayer and meditation, that He will give you direction as to what to do, when to do it, and how to do it. Prayer is the part that keeps you focused on the road ahead. This number one player is what changes things. You have to have prayer and faith that God will show up and give you direction for your life.

We already referenced that the steps of a good man are ordered by God. However, if you are not praying, He cannot order your footsteps. My prayer life is intact, but, like anything else, there is always room for improvement. This is why I am always trying to do more. The more you do, the better the results will be. The more you pray, the more you read the Word, and the more you're around praying people, the closer you get to God and the clearer His voice becomes.

It is also good to have people praying for you. God has a way of placing people in your life to do that. One such person for me is Pastor John Nash. It seems like God would have him to call me at times when I really needed someone to pray for me. There have been many times when he would just call and say, "Does anybody need any prayer today?" He has been doing that since we met in the late 80s or early 90s, and that means so much to me.

The Bible says that the prayers of the righteous availeth much (James 5:16). If you are living right as best as you know how and your heart is right towards God and people, He is obligated to answer your prayers. However, we must have a clean heart. The Amplified Version of the Bible says in Jeremiah 17:9 that the heart is deceitful and extremely sick. David knew this, which is why he so earnestly asked God to give him a clean heart in Psalm 51. It is just as important for us to ask God to create a clean heart in us so that our heart will be right toward God and people. And when we find ourselves in the midst of the many "whatevers" of life, we should know that He might not come when we think He should come, but He's always on time. Sometimes if God doesn't answer our prayers the way we think He should, it could be that He's shielding us from making a bad decision. And that's just the attitude that we have to have. His ways are not our ways and His thoughts are not our thoughts.

We have to accept whatever God gives us in our time of prayer and fellowship with Him. When we do this, we will find that He will reveal Himself and His plans for our life. I have found this to be true many times over. A case in point is a project that I am working on as we speak. It is concerning a piece of dirt (property) that I saw about five years ago in the City of Fayetteville. I called the owners and expressed my interest in possibly buying it. I later discovered that they had eventually put it on the market. After waking up one morning and taking a look at the different rents that I pay (at our various locations), I said to God, "Well, Lord. This rent is getting higher and higher and higher. Do you want me to continue on with this?" I was asking Him for direction. He brought back to my mind that piece of dirt that I previously referenced. It's only about half a mile from my current Fayetteville location.

I started the process of inquiring about the property, and I learned that a couple of restaurateurs (Cookout and Jimmy Johns) had already started trying to purchase the property, but neither deal went through. I reached out to a friend of mine, Emery Shane, who also happens to be in the real estate business. After he checked on the property, he was able to secure a contract on that piece of land on my behalf. This is one of the reasons why I am so grateful for having good relationships. My friend is not simply a real estate investor; he is anointed at what he does. Because of the presence of the Holy Ghost in his life, God used him to be able to make a point of connection that I may not have been able to make. I do believe this was because of the relationship he already had with the selling agent. However, I also believe that if I did make the connection, they may have chosen not to work with me. Most importantly, God showed me that if I had gone on my own and pursued the property when I first thought about it, doing so would not have been a good move to make.

This only reinforced the truth that it's not always about the money you may have; it's about the relationships. Whatever you are pursuing is for you; God already has it worked out because it is pre-ordained. Don't mess it up. Just try to hear from God. If I had been anxious, I might have pursued the property prematurely. That's why the Bible says to be anxious for nothing. I have been through enough experiences to the point where I now understand to call on the Lord and tell Him, "I've done all I can do at this point," when times of uncertainty arise. It's nothing for me to tell Him, "I need you to work it out." He already knows what the future is going to bring. If I push my way in and it's not designed for me to be in, I could be pushing myself into something problematic.

This is why we need to let our footsteps be ordered by God. We have to learn to wait on the Lord. It takes wisdom to wait on God and watch Him work. As of this writing, the deal has been completed, but there were times in the transaction where the devil was in the details. He had gotten in to the mix and tried to make us believe this was not going to happen. The civil engineer didn't want to go any further until he knew that the matter at hand was under control. In short, he brought to our attention that there is a ditch that runs behind the property. We needed to know whether or not the City had control of the water and whether or not we needed to get a different type of approval.

The City had called a meeting pertaining to the site one particular day. I found out about the meeting an hour after I left the site. I had made it to my destination downtown and there was no way I could get back to the meeting in time. I said, "Lord, you have to do it anyway. If it is not your will, it won't be done." I asked God to handle it; I would know if it was His will, then this issue would go away. We wouldn't have to make other decisions about this water issue.   As God would have it, my son was already on the property. He had business there because the owner of the property had given us the okay to put the food truck there and sell if we desired to. Theredore, when my son called me and told me that the City officials had come to the property, I told him to go out there, give them his card, and ask them how things looked. They told him everything looked good. They told him that the water would not be a problem for this site. Praise God!

When I got back on the south side of town, Emery had just sent the email that he read to me. The water issue was a distraction, but God gave a confirmation to let us know that we were on the right track with this deal.   We realized that this was a distraction because of the blessing that the new location will be. You see, the people that I consult with told me the new location will be better than our current location; we should conservatively see a 5-10% increase in sales. God ordered it, and I am so happy to see that God has brought it to pass. It is important to have as close a walk with God as you can because the devil is fighting for the same space that God has in your life. When you have God, the devil is mad and he will do all he can to come against what God is doing.

Just as important as prayer and having a relationship with God are the ways in which we give unto the Lord, as well as the time that we take to worship Him. I understand that many people have struggles with the giving of their financial resources. When I didn't have anything, I still tried to give to the best of my ability. After I was saved and learned about God's way of how He would have me to give, I would tithe on what I brought home. I have never been debt-free in the business, but I believe it's coming. I do get a paycheck every week and I tithe off it. Whatever the Lord allows me to take for personal use, I tithe on that.

When it comes to giving, I always make sacrifices by the leading of the Lord in the community, in the church, in my family, with employees, friends, and where ever God leads me. Luke 6:38 says that when we give, it shall be given back to us. It will come back with good measure, pressed down, shaken together and running over shall men give back into our bosom. This is good news. However, we should understand that it is just as important to have the heart to give. It's not good to give grudgingly because God loves a cheerful giver (2 Corinthians 9:7). Sometimes you may not have it to give, but I have experienced that this is when it means the most.

I used to think about giving from the perspective of giving until it hurts. I have done that, but I have also learned that you have to exercise wisdom and discernment when giving. There will be times when you give to people, but they won't even appreciate what you have given. It is unfortunate that sometimes people feel like you are obligated to them simply because they have assumed you have it to give. God has shown me that He will choose to whom you are to give; to whom you are to help. If you have the right heart, you'll be free in your spirit of giving. As a result, I have given as God would have me to give. He hasn't given me money to stack to the ceiling, but He has always met my needs.

I do believe that there is truth in the statement that says, "Image is everything." Therefore, I try to portray an image of abundance because, from an economic or marketing perspective, that is what people are drawn to. As a businessperson, if you want to create sales, you have to look the part.

You have to present yourself in such a way that portrays you of being worthy of the dollars you are endeavoring to generate. I am appreciative of the fact that God has allowed me to build the brand in such a way that it appears we are over the top, but the truth of the matter is that I'm not somewhere sitting in an ivory tower. I'm still very much in the struggle. I work hard every day to be the best I can possibly be.

The more I think about it, the more I realize how much I cannot afford not to walk closely with God. Every day is an opportunity to get closer to Him, and this includes making sure that I take time to be regularly involved in worship. I know of many leaders who refrain from attending worship services. This could be attributed to demanding schedules. Then again, it could be attributed to an attitude that has caused them to simply be okay with not going to church.

While I am not judging anyone, I do know that God's Word instructs us in Hebrews 10:25 to refrain from not assembling ourselves. In other words, that verse encourages us to attend worship services regularly. God is not a respecter of persons; this verse is speaking to all His children, regardless of their status. You have to make time for worship and prayer. If you are in the right house where the true Word of God comes forth, there's something created in the atmosphere. At Word of Faith, the Lord dwells in the sanctuary, and you can feel the presence of the Lord if you have that kind of relationship with Him. The teachings that Bishop Bronner brings forward are so very powerful and extraordinary that they will literally bring you up out of your seat when the Word hits you.

I know for myself that you have got to be in the house of God in order to take in all that He has for you. There are times on Sunday mornings when I may say, "I'm just going to stay home today." On those occasions, which are not frequent, my wife will say, "No. Let's go." My reasoning is not that I don't feel the need to go, but sometimes my body may simply be tired and I feel the need to rest. Nevertheless, when I concede and go on, I always feel so much better. The Word has a way of strengthening you and pushing you so you can go a bit further.

The faith factor has drawn me closer to God by strengthening my prayer life, teaching me how to give, and showing me the importance of making the time to go to God's house and give Him the praise of which

He is so worthy. My faith factor has also allowed me to experience miracles in my life. One such miracle occurred in the late 1980s. I had not been saved very long, and I remember picking up some paper supplies from a location near Fulton Industrial Boulevard. I was at the red light in an old blue step van. As I was waiting for the light to change, a semi-truck ran the red light. The only thing I could think to do was to slam on the brakes, but when I did, my foot slipped off the brake back onto the gas pedal. And the van just stood still, which was totally odd and unexpected. Actually, it was a miracle of God that caused the van to stop where I was! The Lord stopped my van after my foot slid off the brake back on to the gas pedal. That, I know, was a miracle because I had just started to proceed and go across the highway. I can't bear to imagine the possibility of what could have happened had the van not stopped. If the van had kept going and thrust me into the middle of the oncoming traffic in the midst of that busy street, the outcome could have been devastating.

After I realized what had just happened, all I could do was sit there in total shock. While I was sitting, I felt totally drained; all the strength and adrenaline in my body was gone. There I was in the middle of Fulton Industrial Boulevard. Somehow I mustered up enough energy to open the door of the van. Even so, all I could do then was lay on the door. Nobody blew their horn or tried to get me to move, and all traffic coming from both ways had come to a standstill. It was like everybody was in awe at what they had seen. I eventually got back in the van. And to my surprise, the van was still just sitting there in drive....it was still on! I got back in the van and proceeded on across the highway.

Another miracle is when God shielded me from what could have been a deadly episode in my life. It happened during the time when I used to go around to the stores upon their closing and pick up money made for the night. I had about two or three locations that I had to do this for. On one particular Friday or Saturday night, I went home to lay down because I was tired. My full intention was to rest for a little while, get back up and go pick up the money. This is what I told Diane I was going to do; she already knew this was my normal routine.

My daughter, Tina, was just a baby, and Diane reminded me that she needed some milk or something.

We were all laying in the bed, and I did something I had never done before. I overslept! I did not wake up until the doorbell rang at approximately 2:00 or 3:00 in the morning. Not only did I miss going to pick up the money, but I also didn't get the baby's milk. On this cold, winter morning, I went to the door only to find the police standing there. He started telling me that one of my neighbors, Ms. Jolly, had seen this particular guy walking around the neighborhood. This was not uncommon for her to notice because she was actively involved in our Neighborhood Watch. What was uncommon, however, was for someone to be out walking the streets that time of morning because most people are sleep at that time. For whatever reason, God had her up and alert. She thought it was strange for him to be walking around on a cold night, so she called the police to check things out.

When the police checked, the guy said that he had been to visit me. As I continued to converse with the police, God started speaking to me and telling me that He put me to sleep because He knew that the young man had an intention of robbing me. As the conversation progressed, we found out that the young man was one of my employees. The real deal was that he was waiting for me to come out of my house, go to the store and come back, but I never did. He told the officer that he had come into the neighborhood to visit me and that he had just left my house. But the more the young man talked, the more he confused himself, and the more the enemy confused him. After the Lord began to minister to the police through me, it became clear that the young man had come to rob me and that he had not been to my house as he had said. The officer locked him up because he had a wooden or iron club in his hand, which is what he was going to use to attack me.

As I think about what happened that night, God is reminding me of how I used to carry a 357 magnum and keep it on the seat of my car. I also used to carry a derringer (small gun) in my pocket. But the Lord told me during that particular time that He had me; that He was my protection. I cried out to Him, "Lord, you put me to sleep and didn't let me wake up. You protected me from this robbery. I had never done that before where I didn't wake up to go back to the store and pick up the sales for the day." (Afterwards, God gave me a different way of handling the money. He showed me I was putting myself in harm's way by going to the store and picking up the money at night.) As I cried out to God, He started ministering to me and telling me that because He was my protection, I didn't need any guns. From that night until this night, I have never carried a gun again.

Those two incidents were most definitely miracles in my life, but there was yet another that I would like to share. Around August 2015, I went to the doctor to follow up on a degenerating disc. I found out about it in 2011 and then I had back surgery in 2012. So, I went back to the doctor in 2015 because the pain I was having reoccurred, and I really needed to find out what was going on with me. One doctor's visit led to the referral to another doctor. Before going to the second doctor, an MRI was ordered. When the second doctor read the MRI, he announced to me that I had some kind of spine cancer. The next step was to send me to another doctor to get a bone scan so we could see if the cancer had spread.

Prior to this happening, I had been asked by Aunt Dot in July to come to Tampa and preach for her 90th birthday celebration. What an honor this would be, particularly since she has been a member of her church for 75 years. After I received the news about the cancer, it weighed on me very heavily. I didn't share the news with my family, so bearing the news was all the more difficult. I pressed my way and preached in Florida on the 30th of August. In the meantime, I kept encouraging myself by saying, "I'm going to have to try to make it through until then." The trip to Florida ended up being a full Anthony family affair. My wife and kids went, and we all came together and really celebrated my Aunt Dot. We spent quality family time together, and when Sunday morning came, we went to church together. It was her heart's desire just to hear me preach again. I was obedient, and from what I understand, many, many people were overwhelmed about the message. To God be the glory!

I got back home that Sunday night, and I made a doctor's appointment on Monday for Friday. Oddly enough, my doctor told me he didn't see anything! "I don't see anything that's cancerous," were his words. All I could do was shout for joy. God later showed me that the reason why it seemed like the devil was trying to steer me from going to Florida and preaching the message I preached and seeing my aunt was because of the life-changing impact that would be made. The enemy didn't want that to happen, but God had another plan. He gave me the strength to pursue it and go forward with it.

I finally told my wife after I went to the doctor that Friday. The doctor looked at the report and called the hospital. The second doctor had sent me to get a bone scan. He said what he thought he saw had spread throughout my body. However, when the doctor talked to the radiologist and read his report, they didn't see anything! GLORY HALLELUJAH!!!! I know the devil is angry. I know he's mad.

He is probably angry at the fact that one of my employees (James Thomas) was led to Christ before he made his transition from earth not long after this time. Pastor John Flott and Elder Chef Frank Wingo went to the hospital one Sunday afternoon while James was in the hospital. They were able to pray the sinner's prayer with him, so we believe that he was saved. When I got to the hospital, they had already had prayer with him. They had just left when I got there. I share this because that was another person that came through this company and got saved. On his dying bed, James Thomas was given the opportunity to get his life right with God. This is only another reason why we can show people what This Is It's! first order of business is. It's for people to hear about God, and get their life right so they can make the right choice, which is salvation. Remember, through Pastor Ronald Moore giving his life to Christ, God freed him from being a 23-year heroin addict. God also allowed James Thomas, a former employee, to give his life to Him before he died.

That is why the devil is mad with me. Even while in the process of writing this book, I had two accidents. My truck stayed in the shop as a result for more than a month because someone ran into the back of me and tore it up. The very next day after I was hit is when I went to the doctor and God gave me the report of not having cancer. I got a little shook up because I had to go to the emergency room following the accident. Right after that incident, somebody ran into me again. Thanks be to God, I am still here. The enemy must be really trying to make me afraid, but God has a hedge of protection for me to do what I need to do. People's lives will be changed as I live and do what God would have me to do. The enemy already knows it. I'm just amazed at God's protection and continual work in my life.

The miracles God has performed in my life and the extra special touch that He gives me lets me know how much God loves me. I was recently in a board room with eight professionals. I was asked to introduce myself. I marvel at the way in which God will put me amongst people of high caliber and then allow me to start speaking words of wisdom. All these professionals could not believe I had a 10th grade education, that I don't use computers, and that I just tried texting in 2015.

They were looking at me like it's just not possible. The looks on their faces communicated, "You can't run a company that way." Each of them, when they left, left with a different frame of mind. Three of them were saved, and they were just smiling. However, I know the other five were confused. They could not see what God was doing and is doing in my life. God uses me in front of professionals and executives that may perceive me to be less than them. In the midst of Him doing this, He uses me to let them know they are living beneath their privilege. If you don't have a personal relationship with God, if you don't know Him for yourself, you are living beneath your privilege, regardless of the status or title that you hold. The faith factor has taught me this, and I will continue to use it to teach others.

Chapter 12

WHAT I KNOW FOR SURE: LESSONS LEARNED

My life's journey has been incredible thus far. God has allowed me to experience so many things, and with each experience came valuable lessons. As such, I thought it would be great to share with you some of the most valuable, tried, and tested principles that I have adopted as an integral part of my life. They have worked, and continue to work, for me in ways too numerable to count. I hope they will be a blessing to you as well.

1. **Faith factor** – I cannot put enough stress on the importance of faith. The Word of God teaches that without faith it is impossible to please Him. How do we get faith? It comes by hearing, and hearing by the Word of God. Take the time to seek the face of God by reading His Word and by keeping your prayer life active. Talk to God and then be patient enough to wait for Him to speak back to you. This is where meditation comes into play. Yes, you must pray. But you must also be willing to press your way to that secret, quiet place so that you can clearly hear God when He begins to speak back to you. You must consistently press your way to that place because you might not hear Him the first or second time you go, but if you are consistent with your meditation God is going to show up. The key word here is patience. Many times we can find ourselves being frustrated because the manifestation of the success we are hoping for may be taking longer to come forth. Many will

only see our struggles or our failures and seek to discourage us or count us out. Never build your hopes on man; always put your trust in the Lord and count on Him to see you through any and every thing.

2. **Knowing how to treat people right** – The Golden Rule of doing unto others as you would have them to do unto you is certainly a key to success. My personal Golden Rule is, "Do better or more for them than you would expect them to do unto you." I further believe a major factor in being able to live out the Golden Rule is that of having a good understanding of the difference between your reputation and your character. Your reputation is who people think you are, and your character is who you really are. In other words, it is very important for you to protect your character. One way to do this is being mindful of how you handle every situation that comes your way, especially as it relates to dealing with people. Treat people right. Treat them the way you would want to be treated. In fact, as I state in my personal Golden Rule, you should strive to treat them better. This can be difficult to do, especially if they have not been so kind to you. Know that not every person will have good intentions toward you. However, you should ask God for wisdom on how to respond and then trust Him to work the situation out accordingly.

3. **Seeking and accepting wise counsel** – It matters not how much experience a person has. There are times when you will need to seek the counsel of others along the way. Accept the fact that you do not know everything and that God places people in your life for different reasons. Ask Him to show you who is sincerely on your side and who can give you the wisdom needed to address the situations at hand. One of the most important admissions you could ever make is accepting the fact that you cannot go through life all alone. Everybody needs somebody to help them along the way. Proverbs 11:14 reminds us that where there is a multitude of counselors, there is safety. In addition, Romans 14:7 says that none of us lives to himself, and no one dies to himself. This is an

indication that no man is an island. You cannot rest only in the knowledge and wisdom you think you have. Ask God to direct you to those who will impart godly wisdom into your life. The reflection of what people call success is actually the presence of God in your life.

4. **Being open to options for growth** – The definition of insanity is doing the same thing the same way over and over again yet expecting different results. In business, you must take the time to evaluate your performance. Take a look at the things that have worked well. Also, take a look at the things that did not work so well. You want to make certain that you don't simply shove these things under the rug, so to speak. I know that there may be a natural tendency not to talk about them, but the truth of the matter is that you have to. Avoiding them will not make the problem go away. Once you address the challenge, you must then be open to taking the necessary steps that can help your business to grow. If this is not your area of expertise, consider hiring a business development specialist or business analyst. Such professionals are formally trained to help you put the pieces to the puzzle together for your benefit. I was fortunate enough to have someone in my life who had a gift from God to analyze. Through him and the use of his consultative skills, God showed me just how important it is to have someone who has experience in your line of work. I learned that it is better to grow your business slowly in the beginning. You must be cautious in growth. Pay attention to cash flow and project out cash flow during the times that you have to spend more money. There will come a time when spending will come to an end, and you should start getting back money in sales from what you put out as an investment, that is if God's plan and His directions were carried out. However, in order to see an increase from what you have expended, you must be open to options for growth, which include your willingness to work hard and follow the direction of God.

5. **Don't be afraid to take a risk** – The meaning of entrepreneur in

the Greek language is "man of faith" and a "risk taker". This is an invaluable lesson that I learned from my Pastor, Bishop Dale C. Bronner. You are taking risks because you are launching into the deep, embarking upon endeavors that may or may not work. But one thing for certain is that you cannot be afraid to take a risk. Nothing beats a failure but a try. And in business, you can expect to face some failures. The Bible says a good man falls seven times but gets back up again. Disappointments and hardships are a part of entrepreneurship. I don't have enough fingers and toes to tell you how many times I failed. The blessing of it all, however, is that I did not allow failure to kill my dreams or make me give up. At some point in time, you must be willing to pick up the pieces and try again. This may very well require that you take risks. As you do so, always keep in mind that you will never know the outcome of a matter if you never give it a try.

6. **Surround yourself with the right people** – Keep in mind that not every person that comes into your life has come for good purposes. They may be very compelling in their efforts to convince you that they are sincerely for you, but in time, God will reveal. In other words, there will be those who will have you to think that they are with you, but the reality will be that they are not. God will show you who they are in time. I believe the Bible gives such an illustration in the parable of the wheat and the tares. Ask God to place the right people in your life. These will be those who will pray for and with you. These will be the ones who will see the vision, run with it, and offer encouragement, even at times when the outlook may not appear to be so bright.

7. **Know your product** – It is important to know how to prepare and market the product that you represent. Preparation of the product is very important so people can talk about it in a positive way. This is valuable because the first real form of marketing is word of mouth. People will tell one another about the experience they had when they came to your establishment. It's always good to know that your product is outstanding so that people will want to come

back for more or tell other people about it. Always try to improve on your product; make it better as time goes on. There's always something that can be done to enhance what you have. You don't always have to get something new. Just make sure that what you have is the best it can be. Also, keep in mind that your product must be accompanied by good customer service. If your product is a little off and your customer service is right on, you will still win. In my business, I always tell the people – especially the cooks – the customer tastes what you feel on the inside. That's really the meaning of what "soul food" is all about. If you're not feeling the love on the inside, it will make itself known in the outcome of the food. Love is what mama or grandma was feeling on the inside when they cooked you that Sunday dinner. Our cooks should feel the love on the inside in order for people to taste the goodness of the product that they have prepared. It's natural for a cook to want to see a person's expression when they taste their product. Psalm 34:8 says, "Oh taste and see that the Lord is good." In our business, it is important that our patrons taste and see that our food is good as well!

8. **Understand the value of a good name** – I have mentioned several times in this work the importance of having a good name. Specifically, I have stated that it was important for me to get my name right. First, your name has to be good enough to be written in the Lamb's book of life, and then it has got to be good enough to do business amongst men you see every day. This has taught me the importance of having integrity. It has the power to make things that could otherwise be difficult a lot less tedious. There are many lessons I learned through this admonishing, particularly as it relates to money. For example, I can now tell you to plan to pay credit cards off at the end of the month. Try to spend your money in places where you get something back in return. This can be in the form of points, a percentage, etc. One thing about having integrity is that it allows you to be able to do this; you can spend money in places that give you the best benefit of spending your money. Having a good name allows you to use others' money or

use the system's money, and you can do this for a lower interest rate when you need to have the money on a long-term basis. I also learned to keep debt at a minimum; this applies to both business and personal debt. You should also keep assets two to three times higher than short-term debt.

9. **Prepare yourself for the vision** – You must always be mindful of your vision. Write it down and keep it in a place of high visibility so that you will always be mindful of it. The book of Habakkuk, chapter two and verse 2 confirms this. It says that we should write the vision and make it plain. Actually, not only should we write the vision, make it plain, and keep it in a place of high visibility, but we should also commit it to memory. Recite it to yourself daily so you can plant it in your heart. Also, Proverbs 3:5-6 instructs us to trust in the Lord with our whole heart. We should not lean to our own understanding. In all things, we should ask and trust God. Then, He will direct our path. This is the foundation of the roadmap that you will follow to reach your destination of success. But just as important as the visibility of the vision is your finances. The Word of God teaches that money answers all things. This is talking about things that pertain to finances. Therefore, you must know how much money you are working with in order to be able to answer those things that lie ahead of you. Otherwise, you will find yourself wandering aimlessly, going nowhere fast. One way to keep from having such a lack of direction is to have a good understanding of your profit and loss statement, a balance sheet, or other financial statements. The numbers on these statements must literally talk to you. Then you will understand what to do because you have better insight on the cash flow.

10. **Remain humble** – It is very easy to get "puffed up." Some get so caught up in titles, power, and prestige that they begin to feel like they are invincible. This is not God's intention. He resists the proud but gives grace to the humble. This is where I desire to be and remain in my relationship with Him. I realize that without Him I am nothing, I have accomplished nothing, and my future

holds nothing positive. But with Him and through Him, I can do all things. My prayer is that I will forever remain humble. I will always give Him praise, glory, and honor for being the mighty God that He is. Along with being humble comes the task of being accountable. You should be accountable to God first, and then you must also be accountable to someone who will not simply be a "yes mate." It should not be someone who will go along with any and everything you say and do, regardless of whether it is right or wrong. You have to be accountable by paying attention to the ones that are close to you, especially your spouse and those that work closely with you. Even if you are the one who has to make the decision, you still have to listen first and then make your decision. I also try to encourage people never to make a decision the same day a proposition presents itself. Always give yourself some time to ask God if this is the right decision, especially on major deals and major contracts. Ask God to help give you the right mindset that leads you into making the right decisions. This is so important because your decisions play a major part in the life you and others will live afterward.

11. **Recognize the importance of having a marketing budget** – Not factoring in costs for marketing is one of the greatest mistakes that can be made in business. Social media outlets such as Facebook, Instagram, and LinkedIn have presented a world of opportunities for business exposure for little or no cost. Although greatly vital, social media hasn't gotten to the point of strength and power that it can be the only source of marketing. However, there are traditional methods of marketing that must be considered, such as mainstream television, cable TV, radio, print media and direct mail. You have to figure out which one will work best for your products and/or services, and you'll have to be consistent with whatever you choose. Consistency and frequency equals bigger sales. These methods come with a price tag. Failing to include marketing in your budget will cost you in more ways than one. You should keep in mind that you can have the best product or service in the world, but if no one knows about your product or service, then all you have is

just another product or service. This is why effective marketing is so important. You will soon discover that you cannot afford to not have a marketing budget if you expect to grow your business and watch it thrive.

12. **Build cash in the business** – It will not hurt you to sacrifice the luxuries of life at the beginning of your entrepreneurial journey. Making such sacrifices will help you to build cash in the business. In order to provide for yourself, just take the bare minimum of what you need to pay your personal bills with. That which you don't take will eventually amount to something. Every 18-24 months as you build cash in the business, you can give yourself a small reward. If you have gone through a cycle of business – paying taxes and all the other business expenses – your good name will allow you to get credit. Remember, principle 8 suggests you pay your credit cards off monthly, if possible. Don't forget: credit is like fire. It will burn you up if you don't know how to use it. If you have terms with major vendors, you should have cash that will cover those costs. Whereever you have terms, if you're not paying the balance off, you should have cash set aside to cover it. All of this ties in one to another. In business, cash is king. When you build up cash, sometimes you get to a point where you feel like you have to spend money. It's kind of like a hunger pang you may experience when you're trying to lose weight; you begin to feel like you absolutely have to have something to eat or that piece of fried chicken. If you can make it past the hunger pang, you'll be alright. In the same manner, money will build up, and it can be tempting to want to spend. You must have the fortitude to pass it by and not give in to the temptation. Then you can think clearly about how you will make improvements in the family and the business. You never know when the enemy will come and take what you may or may not have. So go ahead and make the necessary sacrifices early on. The good news is that the Bible says that your latter days shall be greater than the beginning.

13. **Find balance (between God, family, and business)** – I'm often

asked how I find balance in managing all the responsibilities with which God has entrusted me. I wish I could say that it was easy, but that would be misstating the truth. The best way to achieve balance is by keeping God first, then family, then business. Doing this is a lot easier said than done, but it's not impossible. It takes time to master this principle, but with God's help and the support of your family, it can be done.

14. **Follow the leading and direction of God in your business ventures** – This principle is so impactful that I had to divide it into mini nuggets of wisdom. As you rely on God for the direction needed, consider these suggestions:

- Always seek God first: Never rely on your own instincts. Seek God in every matter.

- Dream big: Fully understand that there is no dream too big for you. Develop a mindset that says, "Not even the sky is the limit."

- Stay focused: It is very easy to get off course, but you must, by all means, stay focused.

- Work hard: Hard work is necessary, and it will eventually pay off.

- Never give up on your dream: Anybody can give up. Just know that when you make this your choice, you have closed the door for any possibility of your dream to come true.

- Dream bigger than your parents: Most parents desire to see their children go further in life than they did. This can only happen if you have the courage to make it happen by dreaming bigger dreams.

- Dream big in your community: Your community is counting on you to make a difference. Don't forget those who may be less fortunate. Be a light in a world of darkness.

- Keep the dream alive: Every day is a day to add vibrancy to the dream. Do all you can to keep the dream alive.

- The dream that lives on is a part of your legacy: Today, you are reading about my legacy. Do you realize that tomorrow someone could be reading about yours? Keep living the dream. There's a whole world that can be inspired to do their best simply because you lived and because you dreamed.

1. **Know that where ever you are today in life, God still has a plan for the underdog.** – God has a plan for you, my friend. Even if it seems like you are the underdog and that you'll never see the breaking of day or the light at the end of the tunnel, just know that God wants to see you do well. And I'm not merely talking about in the "sweet by and by." I am talking about you being a blessing here and now while you yet live. If you are not sure what God's plan is for your life, seek Him with your whole heart. Ask Him to show you, and then have the courage to do whatever He tells you to do. Always remember that faith without works is dead. Activate your faith and begin to take steps in the direction that will lead you to execute the plan that God has for your life.

Chapter 13

And The Dream Shall Live On

You really can dream a dream that, to some, may seem impossible. You can also conquer that which seems unconquerable. You can face sorrow that seems to be unbearable. And you can run in places where even the bravest would not go.

You can make something right, even if a person is undeserving. You can offer a love supreme. Even when you get tired, you can at least try to reach toward heights unknown.

This is what I desire to do, to reach for those heights. It doesn't matter how hopeless it may seem, and the distance does not matter, either. I will stand up for what's right because I want to make a difference, no matter what the question may be.

The words shared here are a paraphrase of the lyrics to the 1965 Broadway musical, "Man of La Mancha." This song, though penned at a time of impending war, could easily be paralleled to my life. By the grace of God, His unmerited favor has allowed me not only to dream an impossible dream but to live it also. Who would have believed that I – a young Black man in America, a man of very humble beginnings, a man with a minimal education and one who experienced early parenthood – would be where God has allowed me to be today? Truly, I am the underdog. Yet, I am grateful that God has used me to show the entire world that He does, indeed, have a plan for the underdog.

The torch that has been passed from my father to me is now being passed on to my children. Proverbs 13:22 says that a good man leaves an inheritance for his children's children. I believe that to be true. I also believe that in order for the grandchildren to receive the inheritance, their parents (the good man's children) must also receive the inheritance. So when I am asked about a succession plan for the legacy of This Is It! Bar-B-Q and Seafood, I can say with full confidence that the dream shall live on. It shall live on through my children who have chosen to be a part of the business.

The "big picture" of it all is that the business will continue through the leadership of my children in the form of franchising and company-owned locations. It is my hope that God will cause This Is It! Bar-B-Q and Seafood to be represented in every major market of this nation, and even abroad if that is His will also. In the quest to make this hope become a reality, it will be essential that we consciously endeavor to improve on the vision, products, customer service, people skills, and knowledge, etc.

By all means, we must be intentional in every step that we take. Therefore, my priority at this point in time is to ensure a successful transition as my children prepare to take the helm. God chose my oldest son many years ago to be my successor. Telley is an excellent operator. I am grateful that he has mastered the art of operating the stores. The next step is to help him learn not to only operate the stores, but also to run the company. This is of utmost importance because running the company is totally different from operating the restaurants. Running the company has a lot to do with making the right decisions, knowing how to use money, which includes understanding how to read and understand the financial profit and loss statements and the balance sheets. Understanding these statements will serve as somewhat of a blueprint; they tell you how to use the money and so many of the things we talked about in Chapter 12.

Building the right relationships and communicating your vision with all employees, especially your management team, is very important. Your management team will include any business consultants as well as your vendors and your maintenance crew. The maintenance crew is important because they are the ones who keep the equipment in the stores running. The cleaning crew keeps the stores looking good and smelling fresh every day, from the ceiling to the floors. Consultants bring additional expertise to the table, and it should be understood that value is placed upon all people within the operation. From the head of the company to the dish washers, everyone is important.

Another thing is that you have to be aware of everything that you can, including making sure you are doing things at the right cost. Having insight will help you plan for issues before they happen. This is another reason why your steps need to be ordered by the Lord because He already knows. Insight will also show you what needs to be done and how it needs to be done. The good news is that God will give you just the insight you need. Hold on to everything you have learned down through the years. Check and double check as often as possible. Stay close to everything God has entrusted you with, and always know the importance of the people that work for you. This is so very crucial because the people will be the difference makers in the success of the company, going forward. I always pray and ask God to send us people that will represent Him first. In so doing, God reassures me that they can easily represent This Is It!

But again, as far as the succession goes, God has already shown me that Telley (at age 56) will turn over the business to my youngest son, Shelley IV at age 45; and then Telley will consult with him. My sons' relationship will expand from being brothers and colleagues to that of mentor and mentee, just as Proverbs 27:17 references iron sharpening iron. They will both still be in the business, but they will have a richer quality of life than I had. For example, by this time, Telley will be able to enjoy life with his family from a different perspective. As they get older, things should change dramatically concerning all of my children in their family lives. Their responsibilities/balance between God, family and business should really be intact. My hope is that they will be able to spend that quality time with their families. It is not enough for them only to be restaurant workers; my heart's desire is to see them operate as overseers of the empire that God has allowed the Anthony family to establish for His glory.

Ideally, as the business grows, the management team of Jesus and Butch, Inc. and other company entities including franchisees will be trained to provide the employees with a great example of God first, family second, and then the business. This is the formula God has allowed me to follow in my efforts to achieve balance. This includes the benefit of being off on Sundays. That is the first step. The next step will be for neither the employees nor the franchisees not to have to work long hours. This, too, will allow them to have quality time for their families. I do believe that taking this approach will help This Is It! Bar-B-Q and Seafood to continue to be a place where good employees would want to work.

As for my daughters, Tina has already spent a good deal of time working in the corporate office. In addition to working at the corporate office, Tina is also very involved in various aspects of the business. She works in the stores during the peak time of the year, she works on the food trucks from time to time, and she also helps with the catering occasionally. I am also very proud of the fact that Tina is going to school to further her education. However, I knew that there would come a time when she would eventually lead the corporate office; I just didn't know when that time would come. As God would have it, Tina ended up stepping into that position much sooner than expected. This only further proved to me that God has a plan for everything.

Tina took leadership of the corporate office effective January 1, 2017. Prior to this happening, she stood up like a seasoned executive in her conversation during a meeting we had with some outside sources. I was told by one of the attendees that they didn't know Tina had such wherewithal to handle herself so well in that setting. That let me know God was already working. You see, in my way of thinking, I thought this might occur much further down the line; like maybe in 10-15 years. This thought had been pondered within the corporate structure previously, and it was not well-received by one of the associates. Since that time, that particular associate parted ways with the company. Perhaps, God was using the change to further prepare Tina for what would soon come to pass.

Nina's expertise lies more in the day to day operations of the business and customer service. She does a great job from day to day in stores, taking care of the customers, and by assisting Telley and Shelley, IV. She also loves music, writing and singing. My oldest daughter, Consuelo, rejoined the business' marketing department in December 2016. However, she has recently made the tough decision to relocate back to Seattle.

As I bring this work to a close, there is no way I can do so without acknowledging the undying love and support of my wife, Diane. I sincerely thank God for her. Having the support of your spouse is so important when you are an entrepreneur. You need someone who is in agreement with what you're trying to do. You most definitely need to have someone who is on your side for sure. I say this because, as an entrepreneur, you will face so many difficulties. In addition, if you don't have the right kind of support at home, it just won't work. I am so happy and humbled by the fact that my wife, Diane, worked faithfully beside me in the stores for 26 years until my baby girl, Angel, went to be with the Lord. My wife is always willing and able to do whatever I need her to do. She is a very good example of what God meant when He said, "It is not good that the man should be alone; I will make him an help meet for him" (Genesis 2:18.)

Therefore, I just want to thank Diane for all the support she has given me since 1981, which includes helping me to raise my two oldest children. I will never forget praying and asking God to send me one woman that I could be satisfied with. I was such a worldly man at the time – I didn't even know God then – but I recall sitting on the end of some steps and thinking about my situation and my life. God loved me enough to send Diane to me, and I am forever grateful. And the scripture says in Proverbs 18:22, "When a man finds a wife, he finds a good thing.

This is not to say, however, that marriage is all peaches and cream. It hasn't always been easy. In fact, marriage is something you have to work on every day. You work through the good and the bad times. I praise God that my wife has always been there praying for me and helping me with the kids that I already had. Then we started having children together. In the beginning she would bring Nina to the restaurant when I couldn't make it home before her bedtime or dinner time. She would bring her to the restaurant so we could have some family time before Nina went to bed. This may seem like a small matter to some, but it is the simple things like this that help make life sweeter. It takes a special person to offer support in that kind of way. And it always makes a man feel better just knowing that he has someone who is truly in his corner, one that will love him unconditionally, take care of their home and children, and encourage him so that he can keep going. It is even sweeter when she loves the Lord. This is what my Heavenly Father has blessed me with, and I cannot thank God or Diane enough.

With every passing day, I am given the opportunity to witness the faithfulness of God. It is my earnest prayer that the dream will live on. To God be the glory for all that He has done, for all that He is doing, and for all that He shall yet do. Be encouraged, my friends. If you have ever felt like the underdog, another earnest prayer of mine is that you will be able to look at the course God has allowed me to chart and grab hold of hope that God does have a plan for your life. (See the Butch Anthony Legacy in the Appendix.)

Bonus Chapter

Defining Moments

There are moments in time that help shape you as a person. I call them defining moments. A defining moment is when you have to take the bad and make the best of it. Most defining moments will come out of bad or frustrating situations. They have a way of structuring your future; how you choose to respond could either make or break you. I don't know if anyone ever really takes the time to ponder the handling of defining moments, but it is important, nevertheless. How will you deal with them? Will you make the right decisions? When such moments come, you have to really trust God and make God-like decisions. He will raise you up and take you to higher places if you allow Him to do so.

Two of the most poignant and memorable defining moments of my life took place in 2009, wherein my family and I faced the loss of precious loved ones. The first occurred in April of that year, which is when the Lord called my dearly beloved mother home. The pain of losing her was immense, but God gave me the grace to accept what He allowed. He gave me peace that her work on earth was done, and He reminded me that she would want me to continue the work He had begun in me. And so it was.

Just as I was fully embracing the fact that Muhdear was no longer on earth with me, my family faced another tremendous loss. This one, however, was much more devastating than any of us could have ever possibly imagined. You see, I understand that death is an inevitable part of life. We will all have an appointment with it. Because my mother had lived a full life, and because I understood the concept of death, I was able to accept her transition much better than I did when I received the news that came my way in December of 2009. Our beloved daughter, Angel, earned her wings and went home to live with the Lord as the result of an automobile accident. While I understood that death is as much a part of life as life itself, I don't think anything or anyone could have prepared me and my family for this horrific news. This was something that shook me to my very core. It was only the grace of God and the ministering of some of His earthly angels that sustained my family and I during this time and helped us to make it through.

Angel's transition occurred at a time when we were in the midst of building our Panola Road location (in Lithonia, Georgia.) The pain that I was feeling at the time was almost unbearable. It was so intense that I had to stop the construction for a few weeks just so I could gather myself and come to grips with what my family endured.

January of 2010 is when God allowed me to go back to the Panola Road location and begin the construction again. That was one of the hardest things I've ever had to do. It was one of those defining moments of me having to start construction on a project that I just didn't have the strength to do. How could I get through this? I knew I couldn't remain at a standstill forever. But how would I come to myself and pick up the pieces of what felt like a shattered life?

I remember the day I returned to the construction site being a gloomy, cold January morning. The construction workers were there and I knew all eyes were on me. Everyone was watching me to see if I would be able to pull it off. In every building project that I have had, I have always been the visionary. But after 2006, I had to have a contractor in place. Therefore, I still had to fulfill the responsibilities of overseeing the job in order to assure that everything was being built properly.

Every key aspect of the building essentially rested upon my shoulders. To build this building would hinge on my ability to accurately and effectively direct this project. God would have to give me the strength to start the project back up and to complete it because in and of myself, I knew I could not do it.

I was thankful that I could still feel the strength and prayers of those who were supporting me during this difficult time. This was very important because not only was I still grieving the loss of Angel, but only one month prior, I also faced the loss of a dear friend, Rudy Menchan. In addition to being my friend, Rudy had also worked with me for more than 15 years as my building contractor. So at this point, I was facing a double whammy. The team that God had placed around me was aware of this grief because they not only witnessed it, but they shared it, too. We may not have known it then, but God was actually using the team to be just what I needed to make it through.

All that I went through in trying to finish that project was greatly overwhelming, mainly because of the grief that was still in my heart. Nevertheless, God proved Himself faithful. He gave me the strength and the willpower; He gave me everything I needed to complete the job. I shall never forget what He did, and I shall forever give Him glory, honor, and praise. By His grace and mercy, we were able to complete the building and see the opening of it. The joy of the Lord had been restored by His doing.

As I resumed picking up the pieces of my life, God continued to show me favor. For example, I always wanted a Rolls Royce. In 2011, Diane called me and told me she was riding behind my dream car. We had already had conversations about it (as far back as 2008 or 2009 but God hadn't released me to move forward), so her call prompted me to go to the Rolls Royce dealership and ask what it would take to own one. After talking to the sales people, they told me the standards, etc. Of course, they did their research on me.

Not long thereafter, the representative called and told me they had a car that a customer had ordered but was unable to purchase. Because it was during the downturn of the economy, the young man had filed federal bankruptcy. Accordingly, when this happens, you are limited to the amount of money you can spend. This caused the Rolls Royce to become out of reach for the man who had originally ordered it; he was no longer in a position to buy the car.

When I saw the car, I said to myself, "It's not black." That was my first thought because I have always liked black cars, for one, because of their beauty. I am also drawn to them because I am aware that the nature of the restaurant business makes it likely for grease not to be visible over time with getting in and out of the car. Therefore, it has always been important to me to have a black floorboard so that the grease spots would not be easily detected. My youngest son must have read my mind because when he saw the car, he said, "Daddy, we always buy a black car." He was right; but after seeing the two cars side by side, I actually liked the white one better than I did the black one. I was pleased to see that it was just like I wanted it to be. The timing for it all was good, too. You see, at that time, the corporate executives at Rolls Royce wanted a Rolls Royce to be driven in the Black community. Little did I know that God had already made an arrangement for me to get the car. When they called me to get it, I hadn't heard from the Lord yet. So even though the salesman told me I could drive it home that day, I did not make a final decision at that time.

I went home and talked to Diane about it. I also got the kids and let them see it. In a couple of days after I got clearance in my spirit, I went ahead and purchased the car. The Lord told me He was giving me one of the desires of my heart because of how Diane and I handled the way we released Angel to go and be with Him. He also told me that it was because of the way in which I dealt with employees by being closed on Sundays. You see, I made a vow to God in 1997 that going forward (meaning new locations) we would only operate the business six days a week so that the employees could have an opportunity to go to church and spend time with their families if they desired. I held up to my promise.

Our Memorial Drive location was open on Sundays, but God told me to begin to prepare myself for it to be closed on Sundays. He said that when the time was right, I would know it. I missed the first opportunity to close the Memorial Drive location on Sundays in 2008. That was right after we opened our Camp Creek location; that's when I really should have closed it. But as time went on, I didn't see the next opportunity until later.

It's interesting how we may sometimes hear God's voice, but we don't heed to it. I've learned that you just have to move on it, and I didn't the first time I heard Him tell me to close the Memorial Drive location on Sundays. When that time came again, which was in 2016, I put a date on it; November 19, 2016 was officially the last day of Sunday operations for our Memorial Drive location. Shortly before the location closed, I attended a funeral, and someone there ministered to me by telling me that Sunday operations for the Memorial Drive location would be, "Dead, buried and never to be resurrected again."

God is also showing me the need to expand, and has begun to present opportunities for me to go and possess the land. The Word of God speaks of this in Deuteronomy 1:8. I promised Him recently that before I opened another location, our Memorial Drive location would be closed on Sundays. Even though the cost of making this transition is estimated to exceed $400,000 annually, I stand firm in knowing that God is bigger than any dollar we could ever make. Down through the years, He has proven this to be true over and over again. I cannot see with my natural eye how it will all come together, but I do know that the meaning of entrepreneur in the Hebrew is "a man of faith" and "a risk taker," which I learned from Bishop Dale C. Bronner, an extraordinary man of God. Therefore, I just have to trust God that all will be well. And He will, indeed, get the glory out of all of this.

It's interesting that God would speak so much to me concerning His day because another one of my defining moments centered itself around my Sunday worship experience. It occurred at a very pivotal point in my spiritual development wherein I faced a heartbreaking situation at a place my family and I had worshipped for 25 years. It was extremely painful, but all I could do was, again, trust God. Years have passed since this situation took place, and I made certain that I would never discuss the matter until God released me to do so. My primary reason for sharing this is for others to find peace and healing after having experienced hurt from the church. People may render unjust actions upon you, but you have to love them with the love of God, nevertheless. I have come to realize that those who were a part of the situation are human just like I am; we are all subject to have some missteps. To that end, I want those who were a part of what happened to know that I still love them as well as the church. It is the truth that will make us all free.

The situation that I am referencing involved my oldest son, Telley, and his first wife. He was married to my former Pastor's granddaughter. After the Pastor passed away, her grandson became the Pastor. The Pastor's brother was my (ex) daughter in law's father. He and I both served as Associate Pastors of the church.

As far as I knew, my son's marriage seemed to be fine. Seven or eight years prior to writing this book, I learned that the marriage was facing some difficulties. My son did not share the challenges of his marriage with me because he didn't want to feel like he was disappointing me. He only told me when it got to the point where he knew the marriage had become irreparable. I do believe that the Pastor and some of his other family members knew of the marriage's troubles. As I learned more, I further discovered that my son's (ex) wife did not like the business we were in because that was Telley's place of employment, he spent a lot of time there in an effort to help the business to be successful. One thing led to another and it became apparent that she told her daddy that I said something out of terms to her or that I didn't speak to her. We all want to believe our children are always telling us the truth. We want to believe they are perfect, especially when they leave home, get educated, get good jobs, etc. Unfortunately, they are human just like we are; they are not perfect. Naturally, he would believe his daughter. It also made him angry with me.

Unfortunately, the way in which her dad chose to handle the situation was disheartening. He confronted me about it at church, which totally caught me by surprise. The spirit of the Lord told me to hold my peace, so I did not go back and forth with him. Since I felt it was more important not to let this type of behavior go on in the house of God, I didn't say anything. As time passed, I finally decided to speak to the Pastor about it. He basically took his brother's side in this situation as though it was the truth. But there was no truth there at all. I always held the pastor's niece in high esteem, and it was not a good feeling at all to have false accusations made against me. It's even worse when people believe them. This defining moment surely showed me the great necessity of taking precautionary measures with business and family. This is something that was suggested to me years ago by an older businessman.

The situation did not get any better. After a short while, the Pastor's wife, the brother's wife, and their family all turned against me. It was so obvious because of their attitude toward me. However, the most devastating part of it all was when the Pastor stood before the congregation one Wednesday night during Bible Study and indirectly told me to leave the church. I later spoke with one of the church's Elders who was present that night, and he said that he was hoping that I didn't hear that statement. Well, contrary to his hope, I did hear it. The pain that came behind this action was too deep to measure. I could not help but become even more disappointed when I remembered a request that was made of me by the Pastor a few months prior to this happening. He came to me and said the Lord said for me to give $100,000 to the church or something bad was going to happen. He said that if I didn't have the money all at one time, I could pay it in installments.

After he asked me to leave the church, it came to me that he already knew that he and his family would be turning against me. I guess he felt like he had time enough to ask for the money, get it, and then work against me. God wouldn't allow me to give him the money as requested.

Needless to say, this was a very difficult situation. It was difficult, painful, frustrating, and one that caused me and my family to be deeply hurt. But regardless of the feelings this invoked, God used it to give me a whole new insight. It was so sad. It was even sadder to know that the Pastor's grandmother (the church's Pastor Emeritus) had told me years before, "Your greatest hurt sometimes comes from those that are sanctified." That was a statement of nothing but the truth. I can't help but wonder if God had given her a premonition of what was to come. Maybe that was God's way of using her to warn me. We could have never known that one of my greatest hurts would lay in the hands of her grandsons and her great granddaughter. Wow!!!!

You may be wondering how I responded to that defining moment. I had to learn to hold my peace. How could I do that after a false accusation? Couldn't the Pastor just come to me and speak with me man to man so we could get to the bottom of it? I couldn't believe this was happening to me. The whole situation caused me to reflect on my service at the church. Because of my love for God, I made certain that I gave Him my all in every way. This resulted in my extreme loyalty as well as me being the biggest supporter of the church. I did begin to notice that, after God started allowing the business to make some notable strides, I started getting a few negative remarks from the Pastor. It later seemed to be that he and his family members were looking for a cause to have fought against me. This was puzzling because all I wanted to do was serve God in the best way that I could.

I was pained beyond measure because we had spent many years there as members of the church, as servants of God. When Pastor Davis passed away, we had no problem accepting the leadership of her grandson. In our hearts, minds, and actions, we were serving God, not the man or woman servant. Our love for the Pastor, our embracing of the church's vision, and our belief that God's presence abode within the church is what kept us there. Nevertheless, I cannot deny the major role his grandmother played in my spiritual life. She is the one who helped teach me about the church and the power of being filled with the Holy Ghost. She was an extraordinary woman of God whom I shall never forget. To have been falsely accused and publicly humiliated, especially by those who were so close to her, was a very difficult blow to take.

Although I was terribly anguished by what had been said and done, my respect for God would not allow me to fight fire with fire. Sure, I could have gone at it with the Pastor. I could have said negative things about him, and I could have even tried to break up the church. After all he had done, I believe in his heart, he knew it wasn't right. Yet, he still asked me to come to church, stand before the congregation, and tell them how awesome the leadership of the church was. In essence, what he wanted to accomplish was creating a picture that all was well with me, the Pastor, and his family. That simply was not right.

What could he have ever been thinking to ask me to do that? This let me know that he really was confused in his mind. This also caused me to believe that he wasn't at peace with what he had done. This was simply his way of trying to make it right in his heart. But as for me, this was something I just couldn't do. God wouldn't allow it. He showed me that the best thing for me to do would be to take it to Him and leave it at His feet. This would have to be His battle, not mine.

Throughout this ordeal, God kept reminding me of Jeremiah 23:1, which says, "Woe be unto the pastors that destroy and scatter the sheep of my pasture! saith the Lord." The scattering had already been done by what had taken place. God showed me that if I had done "an eye for an eye" and "a tooth for a tooth," I would only be contributing to more scattering. So, not only did God allow me to leave it at His feet, but He also released me to talk about it. I know in so doing, this will be of help to others who have experienced hurt from the church, a place that is supposed to be a place of spiritual refuge.

I still love the people of God, the Pastor of the church, and his family. The Bible says that the truth will make you free. I am free and living and worshiping God at the next level. What a mighty God we serve!

Along with me taking the situation to the Lord came the necessity for me and my family to find a new place of worship. This all took place around 2010 or the beginning of 2011. My family and I left the church in the first quarter of 2011. It is amazing to me that God had already shown me where my new church home would be. He directed me to a church wherein the Pastor (Bishop Dale C. Bronner) had the same qualities of being an extraordinary man of God as was Pastor Davis.

Those two people are the only two people I have ever experienced the quality of "extraordinary" as it pertains to the Word of God and genuine love for people. It is a blessing to know that God loves me and my family enough to direct us to a place of worship wherein we would receive just what we need spiritually.

The defining moments of my life not only embody the challenging situations I have had to face in my life, but God has also shown me unique experiences that have taken place within the business. More specifically, one day as I was standing in the pulpit, God showed me different people who had come through This Is It! and how they eventually gave their lives to Him. He showed me different people from the church I attended (previously), even the Pastor's wife, her mother and sister. He reminded me that He would always take care of me and bless me in this business because I had welcomed God in the business and did not mind Him doing what He wanted to do with it.

Thinking of such things as this makes me feel extremely blessed by all that God has done in my life, particularly in business. It is important to me that I don't take it for granted. I always want to acknowledge God in everything. And as the Atlanta Falcons, whom many people have considered to be "the underdog" in the NFL, prepare to play in the Super Bowl, I most certainly cannot forget to acknowledge what God has done for This Is It! through our divine connection with the team. It was 25 years ago when we were chosen to be the bar-b-q vendor for the Georgia Dome. After some time, I discovered that beer was part of the menu. In my heart of hearts, I knew that I could not have the This Is It! name on the menu and sell beer at the same time. It was just against my standards and beliefs. Therefore, I had to make a decision to step away from us being in the Dome. I just couldn't do it.

I made a conscious decision to call the executive who was in charge of concessions at the time), and I told him I couldn't be involved if they were selling beer. Approximately four to six weeks later, I believe God touched Phil's heart to go and try our product. At that time, we had a location in the West End Mall. Phil stopped by and gave our food a try. God put the taste in his mouth so strong that he called me and said he wanted us in the Dome, and that he would be okay with the Dome not pouring beer out of our stand. This was unbelievable: we were the only vendor in the Georgia Dome that guests couldn't come to and buy a beer! I'm convinced that this was all the Lord's doing.

Some other significant things happened that further cause me to believe that we have a divine connection with the Atlanta Falcons. We were in the Georgia Dome when the Falcons scored their first touchdown and won their first game 25 years ago. And 25 years later, we were with the Falcons again at another level when they played and won their last game in the Georgia Dome, which led to them to be a contender in the 2017 Super Bowl by running a commercial (a very costly commercial, I might add) that aired during that historic and symbolic last game that they would ever play in the Georgia Dome. The only way I can describe us getting the commercial is simply to tell you that it was the favor of God.

I'm not sure if the Falcons even realize it, but I see our relationship as a divine connection; almost like a special covering. I don't believe any of this is a coincidence. I know that God has told me His favor has been with me all of my life. And I just happen to believe that God has a way of allowing that favor to rub off on things, people, and situations that His favored ones are involved in. Surely, having secured an $85,000 commercial at such an important moment in time is nothing less than the favor of God.

Additionally, as this book is being written, we are negotiating a deal to add 100+ locations in the southeast. It hasn't come to pass yet, but as we speak, we've been given a proposal by a major firm that wants to help make this possibility manifest. I just believe that if it's God's will, it's going to happen. It goes back to what God has spoken that we will be nationwide. God has shown me so much, and He has proven Himself over and over again. I have no choice but to trust Him. I do believe that there is nothing too hard for God. He speaks things to me, He presents things to me, and then He either makes provision for them to come to pass, or He will give me godly wisdom on the right choices to make in terms of going forward, rerouting, or cancelling altogether.

I trust Him because I know He only wants the best for me and all that He has entrusted to my stewardship.

The possibility of the 100+ locations introduced me to a new word that I had never heard: PERPETUITY. In essence, this revelation made me realize that the development of these locations could generate income that would never end. Needless to say, I was enlightened. Neither me nor my children had ever heard of this word. Referencing PERPETUITY, my daughter noted on social media that she had learned a new word and that she would never forget it. This new knowledge only inspired me all the more to continue to speak words of life, knowing that words have power. Since perpetuity reflects the possibility for there to be avenues for income forever, then the least I can do is continue to build upon a foundation that will be conducive for perpetuity to become a true manifestation.

I am further reminded of Psalm 24:1, which says, "The earth is the Lord's and the fullness thereof; the world, and they that dwell therein." How can man separate God from what's rightfully His? I believe that's why America experiences some of its trouble. Too often, we see our country trying to separate God from the government, schools, etc. But you just can't take it away. It would be like me coming to someone's house and telling them they've got to find somewhere else to stay. We are having trouble because it's like we are telling God He doesn't belong in what's His.

I am so grateful for God reminding me of this. It warmed my heart in a way that I just can't explain. It touched me, even more when He manifested what I consider our greatest testimony: a 23-year heroin addict being set free! His name was Ronald E. Moore. After all this young man went through, God allowed Him to become employed with This Is It! His tenure with This Is It! caused him to work closely with John Flott (the young man I talked about earlier as part of my spiritual journey.) John was the person God used to bring him into the business. As time progressed after God freed him from his addiction, he was able to remarry his wife, get his children back, and own a This Is It! restaurant. The church he was attending, Welcome All Community

Church, made him the Assistant Pastor over time, and when his Pastor died some years later, the organization made him the Pastor of the church. When Pastor Moore passed away in 2014, the church named John Flott the Pastor. God keeps on proving Himself through This Is It!, and I just can't say it enough: What a mighty God we serve!

After Pastor Moore's passing, it was so wonderful to see the number of people who took the time to come from everywhere ---- from different parts of the country. They were of all races; we saw Blacks, Whites, Hispanics, and probably even more. Their common cause was to celebrate this great man of God's life. The Lord showed me that He allowed Pastor Moore and me to have a divine connection. I told him a few years before at one of his Pastor's appreciation celebrations that God said we would forever be connected. I know, beyond the shadow of a doubt, that he was one of God's miracles here on earth. Because of the journey that he had traveled, God ended up freeing me, him, and others through our This Is It! experience. It warms my heart for people to call me – some even send letters – and thank me for This Is It! being a part of their life. To God be all the glory!

June 21, 2016

Dear Butch,

I come to ask for your forgiveness for the wrong I did many years ago when I was employed by you. I was not aware at the time that you were a servant of God living in your purpose at the time, but you where and still are a man of God. You could have fired me or even pressed charges against me and you did not. Please forgive me for taking money from your establishment that you trusted me with. I was in a very dark place in my life at the time and thought because I went to church I was saved Christian. Making no excuses for my actions, I was wrong and would like the opportunity to apologize with my whole heart. I hope I have the chance to say this to you face to face, but I am not sure if our timing will be the same today, I trust in God for His will to be complete in my life.

I am seeking to go to a higher level in Gods' Kingdom, The Holy Spirit has brought you back to my remembrance many times and I know this must be done before I leave this earth. I am ashamed of how satan had his hands all over me. Looking back, I was deep in sin, a great disappointment to you and was blessed to work for a man like you. The word says confront your accusers. You were correct, I stole from you. I am so, so sorry. Please forgive me, please.

Please accept the enclosed money as an amends to what I took from you. I am not sure of the amount, it was so long ago, I hope this will suffice. ($1,000.00) I ask that you please forgive me and pray for me. I too am a servant of our Lord and Savior, Jesus Christ now. I too am now living in my purpose for 11 years now self employed as an insurance agent. Jesus is the CEO of my company too. You are a great example for so many in so many ways Butch. You planted seeds on fertile ground and it too root many years later in my life. I thank God for you and your position in the Kingdom. I pray that I have your forgiveness and your blessings. My God continue to bless you and all you do. Thank you once again for your Unconditional Love you shared with me.

Sincerely asking for your forgiveness,

SHELLEY "BUTCH" ANTHONY'S CHILDREN AND GRANDCHILDREN

"And he shall be like a tree
planted by the rivers of water,
that bringeth forth his fruit in his season;
his leaf also shall not wither;
and whatsoever he doeth shall prosper."

Psalm 1:3

Photos

My mother, Lillian "Muhdear" Anthony, celebrating after winning a prestigious award at a dinner party.

My father, Shelley "Buddy" Anthony, out on the town at a social event.

Muhdear celebrates a birthday.

A very classy Muhdear coming into her own.

The Young King.

I was crowned king at a school function, and then my mother always told me I was born to be a king.

My parents celebrating my brother's (LaGrant's) graduation from Iowa State University's Law School.

My parents with the graduate.

Muhdear, LaGrant and I.

Aunt Dot (the longest living member of the Anthony family), LaGrant and Muhdear.

Aunt Dot. At the time of this writing, she was 91, in her right mind and has the use of all her limbs.

The young Shelley "Butch" Anthony family with Mr. Anthony's niece, Monique Anthony, at her christening.

Time spent with Uncle Sam (from Chicago), who stopped in to check in on us to impart the meaning of being an Anthony.

Shelley "Butch" Anthony IV's first year as a Western Kentucky Hilltopper. Shelley IV is pictured with his brother, Telley, and cousins Nathaniel and Joshua.

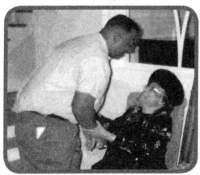

Pastor Lena Davis, the one that drew me to Christ. She always prayed for me and was always on my side.

The Anthony kids: Butch and Diane's young family on our way to church for my niece Monique's christening.

Consuelo graduating from high school.

Birthday celebrations are big in our family.
Shown here with Diane is Rudy Menchan,
my friend and personal contractor. Rudy
built my old office on Highway 85.

Celebrating Mr. Butch's (Shelley IV's)
graduation.

Enjoying a surprise birthday party given to
me by the family.

DeKalb County gave me a proclamation on 8/22, which was also
my dad's and grandfather's birthdays.

Diane having a wonderful day at our first location.

The building of the very first BBQ pit. The idea was given by God as to how to build the pit.

The hard work continues, but it was worth it all.

Pastor Ron and John Flott with a happy customer casting a vote for us. We won first place in the Atlanta Journal's BBQ cookoff.

This is where I cut my teeth on doing construction work (after the contractor I hired ran away with most of the money.)

Mr. T. is shown here with our first BBQ pit, which illustrates our old method of cooking the meat.

The Anthony men: Shelley Butch Anthony IV, Shelley Butch Anthony III, and Telley James Anthony.

How can you lose when you love to cruise?

Time spent on vacation with Diane.

As you can probably tell, we love to cruise!

Consuelo and I during my visit with her in Seattle.

Family means everything. I'm a proud grandfather!

Grandchildren: Sireena Anthony, Shomari Anthony, and Prince Medrano.

Grandchildren: Sireena Anthony and Sara Anthony.

Diane with grand-baby Prince Angel.

Grandchildren: Will and Sam.

A surprise birthday party for Diane as she turned 46. The theme was, "A Queen for Eternity."

The closest I ever got to a prom was this father/daughter dance that I attended with my Angel.

Sister love: Nina and Angel.

My Angel.

Precious Angel.

Diane and Angel at Butch IV's Western Kentucky (WKU) Football Game.

Angel Lydia Anthony.

Franchises for This Is It Bar-B-Q And Seafood Locations are available through the franchising company.

I Believe This Is It!

To learn more about becoming a franchisee of our Full Service Restaurant Specializing in Bar-B-Q, Seafood and Southern Home Cooking:

Visit: www.IBelieveThisIsIt.com

CPSIA information can be obtained
at www.ICGtesting.com
Printed in the USA
FSOW04n0603130917
38691FS